Modern Critical Interpretations

Nathanael West's
Miss Lonelyhearts

Modern Critical Interpretations

These and other titles in preparation

Modern Critical Interpretations

Nathanael West's
Miss Lonelyhearts

Edited and with an introduction by
Harold Bloom
Sterling Professor of the Humanities
Yale University

Chelsea House Publishers ◊ *1987*
NEW YORK ◊ NEW HAVEN ◊ PHILADELPHIA

© 1987 by Chelsea House Publishers, a division of
Chelsea House Educational Communications, Inc.,
  95 Madison Avenue, New York, NY 10016
  345 Whitney Avenue, New Haven, CT 06511
  5014 West Chester Pike, Edgemont, PA 19028
  Introduction © 1986 by Harold Bloom

Printed and bound in the United States of America

∞The paper used in this publication meets the minimum
requirements of the American National Standard for Permanence
of Paper for Printed Library Materials, Z39.48-1984.

Library of Congress Cataloging-in-Publication Data
Nathanael West's Miss Lonelyhearts.
  (Modern critical interpretations)
  Bibliography: p.
  Includes index.
  1. West, Nathanael, 1903-1940. Miss Lonelyhearts.
I. Bloom, Harold. II. Series.
PS3545.E8334M537 1987   813'.52   86 33459
ISBN 1-55546-051-8 (alk. paper)

Contents

Editor's Note

This book gathers together the best criticism available on Nathanael West's masterpiece, the short novel *Miss Lonelyhearts*. The critical essays are reprinted here in the chronological order of their original publication. I am grateful to Cornelia Pearsall for her erudition and judgment as a researcher for this volume.

My introduction relates *Miss Lonelyhearts* to a tradition of Jewish Gnosticism that West did not know but in which, nevertheless, he takes his involuntary but crucial place. The chronological sequence of criticism begins with Stanley Edgar Hyman, whose interpretation of Shrike remains unmatched. Exploring the conflicting varieties of eros in the novel, Roger D. Abrahams sees Miss Lonelyhearts as rejecting the search for something beyond the self and yearning for a state of sexual solipsism. Marcus Smith, interpreting the book's vision of religious experience by a William Jamesian test, condemns Miss Lonelyhearts's quest as inauthentic. Tracing his symbols of chaos and order, John R. May uncovers West's apocalypse as being only the nihilistic expectation of death.

James W. Hickey attempts a Freudian critique of the novel, in which the destructive relationship between Miss Lonelyhearts and Betty is reduced to an incestuous one. A very different reduction is carried through by Jeffrey L. Duncan, for whom the catastrophes of the book are essentially disorders of language.

For Martin Tropp, there is a thread out of the labryinth of despair that the novel constitutes, in traces of hope, such as the prophetic voices that Miss Lonelyhearts hears in the bar. In a brilliant essay, Mark Conroy analyzes the book as a parodistic scene of typing, where Shrike must triumph.

Douglas Robinson ends this volume with a deeply informed placement of *Miss Lonelyhearts* in our national literary tradition, one that frequently reverses the roles of Christ and Satan. By seeing that Shrike is a kind of Christ also, and Miss Lonelyhearts a curious version of Satan, Robinson catches the Gnostic note that is the novel's undersong.

Introduction

Nathanael West, who died in an automobile accident in 1940 at the age of thirty-seven, wrote one remorseless masterpiece, *Miss Lonelyhearts* (1933). Despite some astonishing sequences, *The Day of the Locust* (1939) is an over-praised work, a waste of West's genius. Of the two lesser fictions, *The Dream Life of Balso Snell* (1931) is squalid and dreadful, with occasional passages of a rancid power, while *A Cool Million* (1934), though an outrageous parody of American picaresque, is a permanent work of American satire and seems to me underpraised. To call West uneven is therefore a litotes; he is a wild medley of magnificent writing and inadequate writing, except in *Miss Lonelyhearts* which excels *The Sun Also Rises, The Great Gatsby,* and even *Sanctuary* as the perfected instance of a negative vision in modern American fiction. The greatest Faulkner, of *The Sound and the Fury, As I Lay Dying, Absalom, Absalom!* and *Light in August,* is the only American writer of prose fiction in this century who can be said to have surpassed *Miss Lonelyhearts*. West's spirit lives again in *The Crying of Lot 49* and some sequences in *Gravity's Rainbow,* but the negative sublimity of *Miss Lonelyhearts* proves to be beyond Pynchon's reach, or perhaps his ambition.

West, born Nathan Weinstein, is a significant episode in the long and tormented history of Jewish Gnosticism. The late Gershom Scholem's superb essay, "Redemption Through Sin," in his *The Messianic Idea in Judaism,* is the best commentary I know upon *Miss Lonelyhearts*. I once attempted to convey this to Scholem, who shrugged West off, quite properly from Scholem's viewpoint, when I remarked to him that West was manifestly a Jewish anti-Semite, and admitted that there were no allusions to Jewish esotericism or Kabbalah in his works. Nevertheless, for the stance of literary criticism, Jewish Gnosticism, as defined by Scholem, is the most illuminating context in which to study West's novels. It is a melancholy paradox that West, who did not wish to be Jewish in any way at all, remains the most indisputably Jewish

1

writer yet to appear in America, a judgment at once aesthetic and moral. Nothing by Bellow, Malamud, Philip Roth, Mailer, or Ozick can compare to *Miss Lonelyhearts* as an achievement. West's Jewish heir, if he has one, may be Harold Brodkey, whose recent *Women and Angels,* excerpted from his immense novel-in-progress, can be regarded as another powerful instance of Jewish Gnosis, free of West's hatred of his own Jewishness.

Stanley Edgar Hyman, in his pamphlet on West (1962), concluded that, "His strength lay in his vulgarity and bad taste, his pessimism, his nastiness." Hyman remains West's most useful critic, but I would amend this by observing that these qualities in West's writing emanate from a negative theology, spiritually authentic, and given aesthetic dignity by the force of West's eloquent negations. West, like his grandest creation, Shrike, is a rhetorician of the abyss, in the tradition of Sabbatian nihilism that Scholem has expounded so masterfully. One thinks of ideas such as "the violation of the Torah has become its fulfillment, just as a grain of wheat must rot in the earth" or such as Jacob Frank's: "We are all now under the obligation to enter the abyss." The messianic intensity of the Sabbatians and Frankists results in a desperately hysterical and savage tonality which prophesies West's authentically religious book, *Miss Lonelyhearts*, a work profoundly Jewish but only in its negations, particularly the negation of the normative Judaic assumption of total sense in everything, life and text alike. *Miss Lonelyhearts* takes place in the world of Freud, where the fundamental assumption is that everything already has happened, and that nothing can be made new because total sense has been achieved, but then repressed or negated. Negatively Jewish, the book is also negatively American. Miss Lonelyhearts is a failed Walt Whitman (hence the naming of the cripple as Peter Doyle, Whitman's pathetic friend) and a fallen American Adam to Shrike's very American Satan. Despite the opinions of later critics, I continue to find Hyman's argument persuasive, and agree with him that the book's psychosexuality is marked by a repressed homosexual relation between Shrike and Miss Lonelyhearts. Hyman's Freudian observation that all the suffering in the book is essentially female seems valid, reminding us that Freud's "feminine masochism" is mostly encountered among men, according to Freud himself. Shrike, the butcherbird impaling his victim, Miss Lonelyhearts, upon the thorns of Christ, is himself as much an instance of "feminine masochism" as his victim. If Miss Lonelyhearts is close to pathological frenzy, Shrike is also consumed by religious hysteria, by a terrible nostalgia for God.

The book's bitter stylistic negation results in a spectacular verbal economy, in which literally every sentence is made to count, in more than one sense of "count." Freud's "negation" involves a cognitive return of the repressed, here through West's self-projection as Shrike, spit out but not disavowed. The same Freudian process depends upon an affective continuance of repression, here by West's self-introjection as Miss Lonelyhearts, at once West's inability to believe and his disavowed failure to love. Poor Miss Lonelyhearts, who receives no other name throughout the book, has been destroyed by Shrike's power of Satanic rhetoric before the book even opens. But then Shrike has destroyed himself first, for no one could withstand the sustained horror of Shrike's impaling rhetoric, which truly can be called West's horror:

"I am a great saint," Shrike cried, "I can walk on my own water. Haven't you ever heard of Shrike's Passion in the Luncheonette, or the Agony in the Soda Fountain? Then I compared the wounds in Christ's body to the mouths of a miraculous purse in which we deposit the small change of our sins. It is indeed an excellent conceit. But now let us consider the holes in our own bodies and into what these congenital wounds open. Under the skin of man is a wondrous jungle where veins like lush tropical growths hang along over-ripe organs and weed-like entrails writhe in squirming tangles of red and yellow. In this jungle, flitting from rock-gray lungs to golden intestines, from liver to lights and back to liver again, lives a bird called the soul. The Catholic hunts this bird with bread and wine, the Hebrew with a golden ruler, the Protestant on leaden feet with leaden words, the Buddhist with gestures, the Negro with blood. I spit on them all. Phooh! And I call upon you to spit. Phooh! Do you stuff birds? No, my dears, taxidermy is not religion. No! A thousand times no. Better, I say unto you, better a live bird in the jungle of the body than two stuffed birds on the library table."

I have always associated this great passage with what is central to West: the messianic longing for redemption, through sin if necessary. West's humor is almost always apocalyptic, in a mode quite original with him, though so influential since his death that we have difficulty seeing how strong the originality was. Originality, even in comic writing, becomes a difficulty. How are we to read the most outrageous of the letters sent to Miss Lonelyhearts, the one written by the sixteen-year-old girl without a nose?

I sit and look at myself all day and cry. I have a big hole in the middle of my face that scares people even myself so I cant blame the boys for not wanting to take me out. My mother loves me, but she crys terrible when she looks at me.

What did I do to deserve such a terrible bad fate? Even if I did do some bad things I didnt do any before I was a year old and I was born this way. I asked Papa and he says he doesnt know, but that maybe I did something in the other world before I was born or that maybe I was being punished for his sins. I dont believe that because he is a very nice man. Ought I commit suicide?

Sincerely yours,
Desperate

Defensive laughter is a complex reaction to grotesque suffering. In his 1928 essay on humor, Freud concluded that the above-the-I, the superego, speaks kindly words of comfort to the intimidated ego, and this speaking is humor, which Freud calls "the triumph of narcissism, the ego's victorious assertion of its own invulnerability." Clearly, Freud's "humor" does not include the Westian mode. Reading Desperate's "What did I do to deserve such a terrible bad fate?," our ego knows that it is defeated all the time, or at least is vulnerable to undeserved horror. West's humor has *no* liberating element whatsoever, but is the humor of a vertigo ill-balanced on the edge of what ancient Gnosticism called the *kenoma,* the cosmological emptiness.

II

Shrike, West's superb Satanic tempter, achieves his apotheosis at the novel's midpoint, the eighth of its fifteen tableaux, accurately titled "Miss Lonelyhearts in the Dismal Swamp." As Miss Lonelyhearts, sick with despair, lies in bed, the drunken Shrike bursts in, shouting his greatest rhetorical set piece, certainly the finest tirade in modern American fiction. Cataloging the methods that Miss Lonelyhearts might employ to escape out of the Dismal Swamp, Shrike begins with a grand parody of the later D. H. Lawrence, in which the vitalism of *The Plumed Serpent* and *The Man Who Died* is carried into a gorgeous absurdity, a heavy sexuality that masks Shrike's Satanic fears of impotence:

"You are fed up with the city and its teeming millions. The ways and means of men, as getting and lending and spending, you lay waste your inner world, are too much with you. The bus takes too long, while the subway is always crowded. So what do you do? So you buy a farm and walk behind your horse's moist behind, no collar or tie, plowing your broad swift acres. As you turn up the rich black soil, the wind carries the smell of pine and dung across the fields and the rhythm of an old, old work enters your soul. To this rhythm, you sow and weep and chivy your kine, not kin or kind, between the pregnant rows of corn and taters. Your step becomes the heavy sexual step of a dance-drunk Indian and you tread the seed down into the female earth. You plant, not dragon's teeth, but beans and greens."

Confronting only silence, Shrike proceeds to parody the Melville of *Typee* and *Omoo,* and also Somerset Maugham's version of Gauguin in *The Moon and Sixpence:*

> "You live in a thatch hut with the daughter of a king, a slim young maiden in whose eyes is an ancient wisdom. Her breasts are golden speckled pears, her belly a melon, and her odor is like nothing so much as a jungle fern. In the evening, on the blue lagoon, under the silvery moon, to your love you croon in the soft sylabelew and vocabelew of her langorour tongorour. Your body is golden brown like hers, and tourists have need of the indignant finger of the missionary to point you out. They envy you your breech clout and carefree laugh and little brown bride and fingers instead of forks. But you don't return their envy, and when a beautiful society girl comes to your hut in the night, seeking to learn the secret of your happiness, you send her back to her yacht that hangs on the horizon like a nervous racehorse. And so you dream away the days, fishing, hunting, dancing, kissing, and picking flowers to twine in your hair."

As Shrike says, this is a played-out mode, but his savage gusto in rendering it betrays his hatred of the religion of art, of the vision that sought a salvation in imaginative literature. What Shrike goes on to chant is an even more effective parody of the literary stances West rejected. Though Shrike calls it "Hedonism," the curious amalgam here of Hemingway and Ronald Firbank, with touches of Fitzgerald and the earlier Aldous Huxley, might better be named an aesthetic stoicism:

> "You dedicate your life to the pursuit of pleasure. No over-indulgence, mind you, but knowing that your body is a pleasure machine, you treat it carefully in order to get the most out of it. Golf as well as booze, Philadelphia Jack O'Brien and his chestweights as well as Spanish dancers. Nor do you neglect the pleasures of the mind. You fornicate under pictures by Matisse and Picasso, you drink from Renaissance glassware, and often you spend an evening beside the fireplace with Proust and an apple. Alas, after much good fun, the day comes when you realize that

soon you must die. You keep a stiff upper lip and decide to give a last party. You invite all your old mistresses, trainers, artists and boon companions. The guests are dressed in black, the waiters are coons, the table is a coffin carved for you by Eric Gill. You serve caviar and blackberries and licorice candy and coffee without cream. After the dancing girls have finished, you get to your feet and call for silence in order to explain your philosophy of life. 'Life,' you say, 'is a club where they won't stand for squawks, where they deal you only one hand and you must sit in. So even if the cards are cold and marked by the hand of fate, play up, play up like a gentleman and a sport. Get tanked, grab what's on the buffet, use the girls upstairs, but remember, when you throw box cars, take the curtain like a dead game sport, don't squawk.'"

Even this is only preparatory to Shrike's bitterest phase in his tirade, an extraordinary send-up of High Aestheticism proper, of Pater, George Moore, Wilde and the earlier W. B. Yeats:

"Art! Be an artist or a writer. When you are cold, warm yourself before the flaming tints of Titian, when you are hungry, nourish yourself with great spiritual foods by listening to the noble periods of Bach, the harmonies of Brahms and the thunder of Beethoven. Do you think there is anything in the fact that their names all begin with a B? But don't take a chance, smoke a 3 B pipe, and remember these immortal lines: *When to the suddenness of melody the echo parting falls the failing day.* What a rhythm! Tell them to keep their society whores and pressed duck with oranges. For you *l'art vivant*, the living art, as you call it. Tell them that you know that your shoes are broken and that there are pimples on your face, yes, and that you have buck teeth and a club foot, but that you don't care, for to-morrow they are playing Beethoven's last quartets in Carnegie Hall and at home you have Shakespeare's plays in one volume."

That last sentence, truly and deliciously Satanic, is one of West's greatest triumphs, but he surpasses it in the ultimate Shrikean rhapsody, after Shrike's candid avowal: "God alone is our escape." With marvelous appropriateness, West makes this at once the ultimate Miss Lonelyhearts letter, and also Shrike's most Satanic self-identification, in the form of a letter to Christ dictated for Miss Lonelyhearts by Shrike, who speaks absolutely for both of them:

Dear Miss Lonelyhearts of Miss Lonelyhearts—

I am twenty-six years old and in the newspaper game. Life for me is a desert empty of comfort. I cannot find pleasure in food, drink, or women — nor do the arts give me joy any longer. The Leopard of Discontent walks the streets of my city; the Lion of Discouragement crouches outside the walls of my citadel. All is desolation and a vexation of spirit. I feel like hell. How can I believe, how can I have faith in this day and age? Is it true that the greatest scientists believe again in you?

I read your column and like it very much. There you once wrote: 'When the salt has lost its savour, who shall savour it again?' Is the answer: 'None but the Saviour?'

Thanking you very much for a quick reply, I remain yours truly,
A Regular Subscriber

"I feel like hell," the Miltonic "Myself am Hell," is Shrike's credo, and West's.

III

What is the relation of Shrike to West's rejected Jewishness? The question may seem illegitimate to many admirers of West, but it acquires considerable force in the context of the novel's sophisticated yet unhistorical Gnosticism. The way of nihilism means, according to Scholem, "to free oneself of all laws, conventions, and religions, to adopt every conceivable attitude and to reject it, and to follow one's leader step for step into the abyss." Scholem is paraphrasing the demonic Jacob Frank, an eighteenth-century Jewish Shrike who brought the Sabbatian messianic movement to its final degradation. Frank would have recognized something of his own negations and nihilistic fervor in the closing passages that form a pattern in West's four novels:

> His body screamed and shouted as it marched and uncoiled; then, with one heaving shout of triumph, it fell back quiet.
>
> The army that a moment before had been thundering in his body retreated slowly — victorious, relieved.
>
> *(The Dream Life of Balso Snell)*

While they were struggling, Betty came in through the street door. She called to them to stop and started up the stairs. The cripple saw her cutting off his escape and tried to get rid of the package. He pulled his hand out. The gun inside the package exploded and Miss Lonelyhearts fell, dragging the cripple with him. They both rolled part of the way down the stairs.

(Miss Lonelyhearts)

"Alas, Lemuel Pitkin himself did not have this chance, but instead was dismantled by the enemy. His teeth were pulled out. His eye was gouged from his head. His thumb was removed. His scalp was torn away. His leg was cut off. And, finally, he was shot through the heart.

"But he did not live or die in vain. Through his martyrdom the National Revolutionary Party triumphed, and by that triumph this country was delivered from sophistication, Marxism and International Capitalism. Through the National Revolution its people were purged of alien diseases and America became again American."

"Hail the martyrdom in the Bijou Theater!" roar Shagpoke's youthful hearers when he is finished.

"Hail, Lemuel Pitkin!"

"All hail, the American Boy!"

(A Cool Million)

He was carried through the exit to the back street and lifted into a police car. The siren began to scream and at first he thought he was making the noise himself. He felt his lips with his hands. They were clamped tight. He knew then it was the siren. For some reason this made him laugh and he began to imitate the siren as loud as he could.

(The Day of the Locust)

All four passages mutilate the human image, the image of God that normative Jewish tradition associates with our origins. "Our forefathers were always talking, only what good did it do them and what did they accomplish? But we are under the burden of silence," Jacob Frank said. What Frank's and West's forefathers always talked about was the ultimate forefather, Adam, who would have enjoyed the era of the Messiah, had he not sinned. West retains of tradition only the emptiness of the fallen image, the scattered spark of creation. The screaming and falling body, torn apart and maddened into a siren-like laughter, belongs at once to the American Surrealist poet, Balso Snell; the American Horst Wessel, poor Lemuel Pitkin; to Miss Lonelyhearts, the Whitmanian American Christ; and to Tod Hackett, painter of the American apocalypse. All are nihilistic versions of the mutilated image of

God, or of what the Jewish Gnostic visionary, Nathan of Gaza, called the "thought-less" or nihilizing light.

IV

West was a prophet of American violence, which he saw as augmenting progressively throughout our history. His satirical genius, for all its authentic and desperate range, has been defeated by American reality. Shagpoke Whipple, the Calvin Coolidge-like ex-President who becomes the American Hitler in *A Cool Million,* talks in terms that West intended as extravagant, but that now can be read all but daily in our newspapers. Here is Shagpoke at his best, urging us to hear what the dead Lemuel Pitkin has to tell us:

> "Of what is it that he speaks? Of the right of every American boy to go into the world and there receive fair play and a chance to make his fortune by industry and probity without being laughed at or conspired against by sophisticated aliens."

I turn to today's *New York Times* (March 29, 1985) and find there the text of a speech given by our President:

> But may I just pause here for a second and tell you about a couple of fellows who came to see me the other day, young men. In 1981, just four years ago, they started a business with only a thousand dollars between them and everyone told them they were crazy. Last year their business did a million and a half dollars and they expect to do two and a half million this year. And part of it was because they had the wit to use their names productively. Their business is using their names, the Cain and Abell electric business.

Reality may have triumphed over poor West, but only because he, doubtless as a ghost, inspired or wrote these Presidential remarks. The *Times* reports, sounding as deadpan as Shrike, on the same page (B4), that the young entrepreneurs brought a present to Mr. Reagan. " 'We gave him a company jacket with Cain and Abell, Inc. on it,' Mr. Cain said." Perhaps West's ghost now writes not only Shagpokian speeches, but the very text of reality in our America.

Miss Lonelyhearts

Stanley Edgar Hyman

When *Miss Lonelyhearts* was published in 1933, West told A. J. Liebling that it was entirely unlike *Balso Snell,* "of quite a different make, wholesome, clean, holy, slightly mystic, and inane." He describes it in "Some Notes on *Miss Lonelyhearts*" as a "portrait of a priest of our time who has had a religious experience." In it, West explains, "violent images are used to illustrate commonplace events. Violent acts are left almost bald." He credits William James's *Varieties of Religious Experience* for its psychology. Some or all of this may be Westian leg-pull.

The plot of *Miss Lonelyhearts* is Sophoclean irony, as simple and inevitable as the plot of *Balso Snell* is random and whimsical. A young newspaperman who writes the agony column of his paper as "Miss Lonelyhearts" has reached the point where the joke has gone sour. He becomes obsessed with the real misery of his correspondents, illuminated for him by the cynicism of William Shrike, the feature editor. Miss Lonelyhearts pursues Shrike's wife Mary, unsuccessfully, and cannot content himself with the love and radiant goodness of Betty, his fiancée. Eventually he finds his fate in two of his correspondents, the crippled Peter Doyle and his wife Fay. Miss Lonelyhearts is not punished for his tumble with Fay, but when on his next encounter he fights her off, it leads to his being shot by Doyle.

The characters are allegorical figures who are at the same time convincing as people. Miss Lonelyhearts is a New England puritan, the son of a Baptist minister. He has a true religious vocation or calling, but no institutional church to embody it. When Betty suggests that he quit the column, he tells her: "I can't quit. And even if I were to quit, it wouldn't make any difference. I wouldn't be able to forget the letters, no matter what I did."

In one of the most brilliant strokes in the book, he is never named, always

From *University of Minnesota Pamphlets on American Writers.* © 1962 by the University of Minnesota.

identified only by his role. (In an earlier draft, West had named him Thomas Matlock, which we could translate "Doubter Wrestler," but no name at all is infinitely more effective.) Even when he telephones Fay Doyle for an assignation, he identifies himself only as "Miss Lonelyhearts, the man who does the column." In his namelessness, in his vocation without a church, Miss Lonelyhearts is clearly the prophet in the reluctance stage, when he denies the call and tells God that he stammers, but Miss Lonelyhearts, the prophet of *our* time, is stuck there until death.

Miss Lonelyhearts identifies Betty as the principle of order: "She had often made him feel that when she straightened his tie, she straightened much more." The order that she represents is the innocent order of Nature, as opposed to the disorder of sinful Man. When Miss Lonelyhearts is sick, Betty comes to nourish him with hot soup, impose order on his room, and redeem him with a pastoral vision: "She told him about her childhood on a farm and of her love for animals, about country sounds and country smells and of how fresh and clean everything in the country is. She said that he ought to live there and that if he did, he would find that all his troubles were city troubles." When Miss Lonelyhearts is back on his feet, Betty takes him for a walk in the zoo, and he is "amused by her evident belief in the curative power of animals." Then she takes him to live in the country for a few days, in the book's great idyllic scene. Miss Lonelyhearts is beyond such help, but it is Betty's patient innocence—she is as soft and helpless as a kitten—that makes the book so heartbreaking. She is an innocent Eve to his fallen Adam, and he alone is driven out of Eden.

The book's four other principal characters are savage caricatures, in the root sense of "caricature" as the overloading of one attribute. Shrike is a dissociated half of Miss Lonelyhearts, his cynical intelligence, and it is interesting to learn that Shrike's rhetorical masterpiece, the great speech on the varieties of escape, was spoken by Miss Lonelyhearts in an earlier draft. Shrike's name is marvelously apt. The shrike or butcherbird impales its prey on thorns, and the name is a form of the word "shriek." Shrike is of course the mocker who hands Miss Lonelyhearts his crown of thorns, and throughout the book he is a shrieking bird of prey; when not a butcherbird, "a screaming, clumsy gull."

Shrike's wife Mary is one vast teasing mammary image. As Miss Lonelyhearts decides to telephone Mary in Delehanty's speakeasy, he sees a White Rock poster and observes that "the artist had taken a great deal of care in drawing her breasts and their nipples stuck out like tiny red hats." He then thinks of "the play Mary made with her breasts. She used them as the coquettes of long ago had used their fans. One of her tricks was to wear a medal low down on her chest. Whenever he asked to see it, instead of drawing it out she leaned over for him to look. Although he had often asked to see the medal, he had not yet found out what it represented." Miss Lonelyhearts and Mary go out for a gay evening, and Mary flaunts her breasts while talking of her mother's terrible death from cancer of the breast. He finally gets to see the medal, which reads "Awarded by the Boston Latin School for first place in the 100 yd. dash." When he takes her home he kisses her breasts, for the first time briefly slowing down her dash.

The Doyles are presented in inhuman or subhuman imagery. When, in answer to Fay's letter of sexual invitation, Miss Lonelyhearts decides to telephone her, he pictures her as "a tent, hair-covered and veined," and himself as a skeleton: "When he made the skeleton enter the flesh tent, it flowered at every joint." Fay appears and is a giant: "legs like Indian clubs, breasts like balloons and a brow like a pigeon." When he takes her arm, "It felt like a thigh." Following her up the stairs to his apartment, "he watched the action of her massive hams; they were like two enormous grindstones." Undressing, "she made sea sounds; something flapped like a sail; there was the creak of ropes; then he heard the wave-against-a-wharf smack of rubber on flesh. Her call for him to hurry was a sea-moan, and when he lay beside her, she heaved, tidal, moon-driven." Eventually Miss Lonelyhearts "crawled out of bed like an exhausted swimmer leaving the surf," and she soon drags him back.

If Fay is an oceanic monster, Peter Doyle is only a sinister puppy. In bringing Miss Lonelyhearts back to the apartment at Fay's order, he half-jokes, "Ain't I the pimp, to bring home a guy for my wife?" Fay reacts by hitting him in the mouth with a rolled-up newspaper, and his comic response is to growl like a dog and catch the paper with his teeth. When she lets go of her end, he drops to his hands and knees and continues to imitate a dog on the floor. As Miss Lonelyhearts leans over to help him up, "Doyle tore open Miss Lonelyhearts' fly, then rolled over on his back, laughing wildly." Fay, more properly, accepts him as a dog and kicks him.

The obsessive theme of *Miss Lonelyhearts* is human pain and suffering, but it is represented almost entirely as female suffering. This is first spelled out in the letters addressed to Miss Lonelyhearts: Sick-of-it-all is a Roman Catholic wife who has had seven children in twelve years, is pregnant again, and has kidney pains so excruciating that she cries all the time. Desperate is a sixteen-year-old born with a hole in her face instead of a nose, who wants to have dates like other girls. Harold S. writes about his thirteen-year-old deaf-and-dumb sister Gracie, who was raped by a man while she was playing on the roof, and who will be brutally punished if her parents find out about it. Broad Shoulders was hit by a car when she was first pregnant, and is alternately persecuted and deserted by an unbalanced husband, in five pages of ghastly detail. Miss Lonelyhearts gets only two letters about male suffering, one from a paralyzed boy who wants to play the violin, the other from Peter Doyle, who complains of the pain from his crippled leg and the general meaninglessness of life.

The theme of indignities committed on women comes up in another form in the stories Miss Lonelyhearts's friends tell in Delehanty's. They seem to be exclusively anecdotes of group rape, of one woman gang-raped by eight neighbors, of another kept in the back room of a speakeasy for three days, until "on the last day they sold tickets to niggers." Miss Lonelyhearts identifies himself with "wife-torturers, rapers of small children." At one point he tries giving his readers the traditional Christian justification for suffering, that it is Christ's gift to mankind to bring them to Him, but he tears up the column.

Ultimately the novel cannot justify or even explain suffering, only proclaim its omnipresence. Lying sick in bed, Miss Lonelyhearts gets a vision of human life: "He found himself in the window of a pawnshop full of fur coats, diamond rings, watches, shotguns, fishing tackle, mandolins. All these things were the paraphernalia of suffering. A tortured high light twisted on the blade of a gift knife, a battered horn grunted with pain." Finally his mind forms everything into a gigantic cross, and he falls asleep exhausted.

The book's desperate cry of pain and suffering comes to a focus in what Miss Lonelyhearts calls his "Christ complex." He recognizes that Christ is the only answer to his readers' letters, but that "if he did not want to get sick, he had to stay away from the Christ business. Besides, Christ was Shrike's particular joke." As Miss Lonelyhearts leaves the office and walks through a little park, the shadow of a lamppost pierces his side like a spear. Since nothing grows in the park's battered earth, he decides to ask his correspondents to come and water the soil with their tears. He imagines Shrike telling him to teach them to pray each morning, "Give us this day our daily stone," and thinks: "He had given his reader many stones; so many, in fact, that he had only one left—the stone that had formed in his gut."

Jesus Christ, Shrike says, is "the Miss Lonelyhearts of Miss Lonelyhearts." Miss Lonelyhearts has nailed an ivory Christ to the wall of his room with great spikes, but it disappoints him: "Instead of writhing, the Christ remained calmly decorative." Miss Lonelyhearts recalls: "As a boy in his father's church, he had discovered that something stirred in him when he shouted the name of Christ, something secret and enormously powerful." Unfortunately, he recognizes, it is not faith but hysteria: "For him, Christ was the most natural of excitements."

Miss Lonelyhearts tells Betty he is "a humanity lover," but Shrike more aptly identifies him a "leper licker." "If he could only believe in Christ," Miss Lonelyhearts thinks, "then everything would be simple and the letters extremely easy to answer." Later he recognizes that "Shrike had accelerated his sickness by teaching him to handle his one escape, Christ, with a thick glove of words." He decides that he has had a part in the general betrayal of suffering mankind: "The thing that made his share in it particularly bad was that he was capable of dreaming the Christ dream. He felt that he had failed at it, not so much because of Shrike's jokes or his own self-doubt, but because of his lack of humility." Miss Lonelyhearts concludes that "with him, even the word Christ was a vanity." When he gets drunk with Doyle, he calls on Christ joyously, and goes home with Doyle to bring the glad tidings to both Doyles, to heal their marriage. He preaches "love" to them and realizes that he is only writing another column, switches to preaching Christ Jesus, "the black fruit that hangs on the crosstree . . . the bidden fruit," and realizes that he is only echoing Shrike's poisoned rhetoric.

What Miss Lonelyhearts eventually achieves, since he cannot believe in the real Christ, and refuses to become a spurious Christ, is Peter's condition. He becomes the rock on which the new church will be founded, but it is the church of catatonic withdrawal. After three days in bed Miss Lonelyhearts attains a state of perfect calm, and the stone in his gut expands until he becomes "an ancient rock, smooth with experience." The Shrikes come to take him to a party at their apartment, and against this rock the waves of Shrike dash in vain. When Mary wriggles on Miss Lonelyhearts's lap in the cab, "the rock remained perfect." At the party he withstands Shrike's newest mockery, the Miss Lonelyhearts Game, with indifference: "What goes on in the sea is of no interest to the rock." Miss Lonelyhearts leaves the party with Betty: "She too should see the rock he had become." He shamelessly promises her marriage and domesticity: "The rock was a solidification of his feeling, his conscience, his sense of reality, his self-knowledge." He then goes back to his sickbed content: "The rock had been thoroughly tested and had been found perfect."

The next day Miss Lonelyhearts is burning with fever, and "the rock became a furnace." The room fills with grace, the illusory grace of madness, and as Doyle comes up the stairs with a pistol Miss Lonelyhearts rushes downstairs to embrace him and heal his crippled leg, a miracle that will embody his succoring all suffering mankind with love. Unable to escape Miss Lonelyhearts's mad embrace, terrified by Betty coming up the stairs, Doyle tries to toss away the gun, and Miss Lonelyhearts is accidentally shot. He falls dragging Doyle down the stairs in his arms.

It is of course a homosexual tableau — the men locked in embrace while the woman stands helplessly by — and behind his other miseries Miss Lonely-hearts has a powerful latent homosexuality. It is this that is ultimately the joke of his name and the book's title. It explains his acceptance of teasing dates with Mary and his coldness with Mary; he thinks of her excitement and notes: "No similar change ever took place in his own body, however. Like a dead man, only friction could make him warm or violence make him mobile." It explains his discontent with Betty. Most of all it explains his joy at being seduced by Fay — "He had always been the pursuer, but now found a strange pleasure in having the roles reversed" — and how quickly the pleasure turns to disgust.

The communion Miss Lonelyhearts achieves with Doyle in Delehanty's consists in their sitting silently holding hands, Miss Lonelyhearts pressing "with all the love he could manage" to overcome the revulsion he feels at Doyle's touch. Back at the Doyles, after Doyle has ripped open Miss Lonelyhearts's fly and been kicked by his wife, they hold hands again, and when Fay comes back in the room she says "What a sweet pair of fairies you guys are." It is West's ultimate irony that the symbolic embrace they manage at the end is one penetrating the body of the other with a bullet.

We could, if we so chose, write Miss Lonelyhearts's case history before the novel begins. Terrified of his stern religious father, identifying with his soft loving mother, the boy renounces his phallicism out of castration anxiety — a classic Oedipus complex. In these terms the Shrikes are Miss Lonelyhearts's Oedipal parents, abstracted as the father's loud voice and the mother's tantalizing breast. The scene at the end of Miss Lonelyhearts's date with Mary Shrike is horrifying and superb. Standing outside her apartment door, suddenly overcome with passion, he strips her naked under her fur coat while she keeps talking mindlessly of her mother's death, mumbling and repeating herself, so that Shrike will not hear their sudden silence and come out. Finally Mary agrees to let Miss Lonelyhearts in if Shrike is not home, goes inside, and soon Shrike peers out the door, wearing only the top of his pajamas. It is the child's Oedipal vision perfectly dramatized: he can clutch at his mother's body but loses her each time to his more potent rival.

It should be noted that if this is the pattern of Miss Lonelyhearts's Oedipus complex, it is not that of West, nor are the Shrikes the pattern of West's parents. How conscious was West of all or any of this? I would guess, from the book's title, that he was entirely conscious of at least Miss Lonelyhearts's latent homosexuality. As for the Oedipus complex, all one can do is note West's remarks in "Some Notes on *Miss Lonelyhearts*": "Psychology has nothing to do with reality nor should it be used as motivation. The novelist is no longer a psychologist. Psychology can become much more important. The great body of case histories can be used in the way the ancient writers use their myths. Freud is your Bulfinch; you can not learn from him."

The techniques West uses to express his themes are perfectly suited to them. The most important is a pervasive desperate and savage tone, not only in the imagery of violence and suffering, but everywhere. It is the tone of a world where unreason is triumphant. Telling Miss Lonelyhearts that he is awaiting a girl "of great intelligence," Shrike "illustrated the world *intelligence* by carving two enormous breasts in the air with his hands." When Miss Lonelyhearts is in the country with Betty, a gas station attendant tells him amiably that "it wasn't the hunters who drove out the deer, but the yids." When Miss Lonelyhearts accidentally collides with a man in Delehanty's and turns to apologize, he is punched in the mouth.

The flowering cactus that blooms in this wasteland is Shrike's rhetoric. The book begins with a mock prayer he has composed for Miss Lonelyhearts, and every time Shrike appears he makes a masterly speech: on religion, on escapes, on the gospel of Miss Lonelyhearts according to Shrike. He composes a mock letter to God, in which Miss Lonelyhearts confesses shyly: "I read your column and like it very much." He is a cruel and relentless punster and wit. In his sadistic game at the party, Shrike reads aloud letters to Miss Lonelyhearts. He reads one from a pathetic old woman who sells pencils for a living, and concludes: "She has rheum in her eyes. Have you room in your heart for her?" He reads another, from the paralyzed boy who wants to play the violin, and concludes: "How pathetic! However, one can learn much from this parable. Label the boy Labor, the violin Capital, and so on. . . ." Shrike's masterpiece, the brilliant evocation of the ultimate inadequacy of such escapes as the soil, the South Seas, Hedonism, and art, is a classic of modern rhetoric, as is his shorter speech on religion. Here are a few sentences from the latter:

> "Under the skin of man is a wondrous jungle where veins like lush tropical growths hang along over-ripe organs and weed-like entrails writhe in squirming tangles of red and yellow. In this jungle, flitting from rock-gray lungs to golden intestines, from liver to lights and back to liver again, lives a bird called the soul. The Catholic hunts this bird with bread and wine, the Hebrew with a golden ruler, the Protestant on leaden feet with leaden words, the Buddhist with gestures, the Negro with blood."

The other cactus that flowers in the wasteland is sadistic violence. The book's most harrowing chapter, "Miss Lonelyhearts and the lamb," is a dream or recollection of a college escapade, in which Miss Lonelyhearts and two other boys, after drinking all night, buy a lamb to barbecue in the woods. Miss Lonelyhearts persuades his companions to sacrifice it to God before barbecuing it. They lay the lamb on a flower-covered altar and Miss Lonelyhearts tries to cut its throat, but succeeds only in maiming it and breaking the knife. The lamb escapes and crawls off into the underbrush, and the boys flee. Later Miss Lonelyhearts goes back and crushes the lamb's head with a stone. This nightmarish scene, with its unholy suggestions of the sacrifices of Isaac and Christ, embodies the book's bitter paradox: that sadism is the perversion of love.

Visiting Betty early in the novel, aware "that only violence could make him supple," Miss Lonelyhearts reaches inside her robe and tugs at her nipple unpleasantly. "Let me pluck this rose," he says, "I want to wear it in my buttonhole." In "Miss Lonelyhearts and the clean old man," he and a drunken friend find an old gentleman in a washroom, drag him to a speakeasy, and torment him with questions about his "homosexualistic tendencies." As they get nastier and nastier, Miss Lonelyhearts feels "as he had felt years before, when he had accidentally stepped on a small frog. Its spilled guts had filled him with pity, but when its suffering had become real to his senses, his pity had turned to rage and he had beaten it frantically until it was dead." He ends by twisting the old man's arm until the old man screams and someone hits Miss Lonelyhearts with a chair.

The book's only interval of decency, beauty, and peace is the pastoral idyll of the few days Miss Lonelyhearts spends with Betty in the country. They drive in a borrowed car to the deserted farmhouse in Connecticut where she was born. It is spring, and Miss Lonelyhearts "had to admit, even to himself, that the pale new leaves, shaped and colored like candle flames, were beautiful and that the air smelt clean and alive." They work at cleaning up the place, Betty cooks simple meals, and they go down to the pond to watch the deer. After they eat an apple that has ominous Biblical overtones, Betty reveals that she is a virgin and they go fraternally to bed. The next day they go for a naked swim; then, with "no wind to disturb the pull of the earth," Betty is ceremonially deflowered on the new grass. The reader is repeatedly warned that natural innocence cannot save Miss Lonelyhearts: the noise of birds and crickets is "a horrible racket" in his ears; in the woods, "in the deep shade there was nothing but death—rotten leaves, gray and white fungi, and over everything a funereal hush." When they get back to New York, "Miss Lonelyhearts knew that Betty had failed to cure him and that he had been right when he had said that he could never forget the letters." Later, when Miss Lonelyhearts is a rock and leaves Shrike's party with Betty, he tries to create a miniature idyll of innocence by taking her out for a strawberry soda, but it fails. Pregnant by him and intending to have an abortion, Betty remains nevertheless in Edenic innocence; Miss Lonelyhearts is irretrievably fallen, and there is no savior who can redeem.

The book's pace is frantic and its imagery is garish, ugly, and compelling. The letters to Miss Lonelyhearts are "stamped from the dough of suffering with a heart-shaped cookie knife." The sky looks "as if it had been rubbed with a soiled eraser." A bloodshot eye in the peephole of Delehanty's glows "like a ruby in an antique iron ring." Finishing his sermon to the "intelligent" girl, Shrike "buried his triangular face like the blade of a hatchet in her neck." Miss Lonelyhearts's tongue is "a fat thumb," his heart "a congealed lump of icy fat," and his only feeling "icy fatness." Goldsmith, a colleague at the paper, has cheeks "like twin rolls of smooth pink toilet paper." Only the imagery of the Connecticut interlude temporarily thaws the iciness and erases the unpleasant associations with fatness and thumb. As Miss Lonelyhearts watches Betty naked, "She looked a little fat, but when she lifted something to the line, all the fat disappeared. Her raised arms pulled her breasts up until they were like pink-tipped thumbs."

The unique greatness of *Miss Lonelyhearts* seems to have come into the world with hardly a predecessor, but it has itself influenced a great many American novelists since. *Miss Lonelyhearts* seems to me one of the three finest American novels of our century. The other two are F. Scott Fitzgerald's *The Great Gatsby* and Ernest Hemingway's *The Sun Also Rises*. It shares with them a lost and victimized hero, a bitter sense of our civilization's falsity, a pervasive melancholy atmosphere of failure and defeat. If the tone of *Miss Lonelyhearts* is more strident, its images more garish, its pace more rapid and hysterical, it is as fitting an epitome of the thirties as they are of the twenties. If nothing in the forties and fifties has similarly gone beyond *Miss Lonelyhearts* in violence and shock, it may be because it stands at the end of the line.

Androgynes Bound:
Nathanael West's *Miss Lonelyhearts*

Roger D. Abrahams

Nathanael West's short novel *Miss Lonelyhearts*, in spite of its brevity, is one of the most demanding and perplexing reading experiences of American letters. This work utilizes a totally ironic perspective while telling a story of a very real moral dilemma in psychologically realistic terms, thereby forcing the reader to sympathize with the title character and to laugh at him at the same time. It is a work of utter despair, yet its ironic approach causes despair itself to be branded ridiculous. Throughout, we are asked to identify with one who cannot himself find identification and whose name we never know.

Our perplexity is compounded by the novel's history. Written in the depression years, yet in a style more characteristic of the twenties, the life view presented seems closer to the era after World War II. Perhaps this is why it is only since the issuance of his collected novels in 1957 that West has received widespread critical and popular attention.

Miss Lonelyhearts is a work primarily concerned with the individual's moral and psychological struggle in a world in which all values are suspect, and all attempts to achieve identity are subject to frustration. It examines many systems of thought and action and rejects them all as illusory. Possibilities of help, perfection, and hope are dangled before our eyes and then dashed on the rocks of disillusion. Even with such successive defeats, the importance of the continuance of the search is never questioned.

In this regard the book seems to be built much like Nathanael West himself—at least the West described by his friend Malcolm Cowley:

> To avoid the danger of being solemn he used to stick pins in his
> dearest illusions. Nevertheless he kept having more of them, like

From *Seven Contemporary Authors* edited by Thomas R. Whitbread. © 1966 by the University of Texas Press.

> a boy inflating toy balloons from an inexhaustible store. . . . He
> was always called "Pep," I don't know for what reason, but
> somehow the nickname was fitting; it seemed to reveal a quality
> of continually wounded and revived innocence, as if he were
> everybody's kid brother.

This pattern of "wounded and revived innocence" suffuses the life of the title character, Miss Lonelyhearts. The wounding and the reviving of innocence are equally important, for without the hope of the innocent the wound will not be fully felt. The presence of adversity, of chaos, is admitted then forgotten; an ideal of harmony must be preserved in spite of adversity and even with the probability that it will never be realized in more than a personal and momentary way. Life cannot be fully experienced by retreat. This persistence of the search in the midst of painful forbearance is a pattern which is communicated in all of West's works. It is for good reason that *Miss Lonelyhearts* appears to be a shaggy-dog story, an elaborate tale about activity which seems to drive toward something, only to be exposed as pointless, frustrated action.

One traditional shaggy-dog story reflects just such a frustration pattern in content as well as form. Two rabbis have searched all their lives for the secret of life. Having read all of the many wise books on the subject and having found no answer, they finally turn to meditation. One day one bursts into the other's sanctuary crying, "I've found it." "You've found what?" "I've found the secret of life." "You what? Tell me quickly; what have you found?" "Life," he said. "Life is like a butterfly." "Life is like a butterfly?" "So life *isn't* like a butterfly."

In *Miss Lonelyhearts* the search is both internal and external. The quest is made by one who perceives chaos both within himself and in the outside world and who experiences the two inseparably in his attempt to find order. In looking he is presented with a number of traditional plans of action — some of society's "dearest illusions." Retreat to nature, mysticism, self-sacrifice, sentimental love, worldliness, and the life of total reason — all are explored, discussed, subjected to the cruelest kind of scrutiny, and then rejected. They are discarded not only because they are vanities and hypocrisies, but also because they do not fulfill the needs of Miss L to find either an answer to the inequities of the world or a salve for his wounded psyche.

I

Before scrutiny of the details of Miss Lonelyhearts's search, consideration of the nature of the novel is important. Even though such a widely read critic as Stanley Edgar Hyman states that this novel sprang into the world "with hardly a predecessor," the work derives its tone and patterns of expectations from some very important literary traditions. Simply from the point of view of stylistic effects, West owes a great deal to the symbolists and the surrealists. His uniformly bleak, defoliated world shares a great deal with Eliot and many others writing in the twenties. More important, however, the structure of the work develops upon the techniques and expectation patterns of previous types of prose fiction.

Miss Lonelyhearts is a work which centers upon a central character floundering in the midst of an adverse moral climate and wrestling with problems of both psychological and ethical dimension. In delineating this situation the book draws upon at least three traditions for its vocabulary and point of view: satire, allegory, and the novel of psychological development. As in so many satires, a moral point of view is developed through the presentation of an innocent in the midst of the corrupt, corruption appearing that much more profound because it is presented by the naive observer. Further, the innocent is shown to be fully as deluded and vain as the corrupt; just as we discover that such satiric protagonists as Gulliver and Candide are the dupes of their own insular systems of thought, so Miss Lonelyhearts is revealed to be deluded by his mystical sentimentalism.

In regard to the moral dimension Miss Lonelyhearts utilizes some of the techniques of allegory as well as those of satire. The novel presents us with a central Everyman type character and a number of "flat," subsidiary characters who vie for his soul. Each of the arguers represents a single point of view, a force which is also part of the inner struggle of the protagonist.

Satire and allegory provide techniques drawn upon by many novels of psychological development, and it is this subgenre which is of greatest importance in the construction of *Miss Lonelyhearts*. This type of fiction centers upon a gifted but incomplete individual and his struggle to become whole. Derived from the confessional tradition, and strongly influenced by Dostoyevski, works in this pattern have provided some of the high spots of the twentieth-century novel. Such writers as Joyce, Kafka, Thomas Wolfe, and Beckett, to mention only a few, have been known primarily for this kind of fiction. In all, interest is focused upon the unformed or malformed mind's progress in attempting to attain balance, satisfaction, and insight into self and the external world. Interest resides in psychic struggle. We are generally presented with an individual who, because of the largeness of spirit and an ability to perceive farther and deeper than others, recognizes his isolation. This engenders internal conflicts, for in order to act on these perceptions the individual must achieve some kind of *rapprochement* with the outside world, must make some kind of compromise and must develop a vocabulary, so that communication becomes possible. He is often shown to have capacities of feeling and perception but an inability to organize and effectively express or act on his insights. Until he can do so, he will not achieve his true identity. The experiences which the protagonist undergoes, and their effect on him, determine whether identity will be achieved.

There are two possible attacks on this problem of identity in this sort of novel. In the "artist as young man" type, the pattern is similar to that of a romance: the hero becomes temporarily isolated from society on an active quest of self and the sources of his being. Such works, generally written in the spirit of retrospection, depict experience as causal and progressive and purposive, leading to the present artist-figure. Internal tensions, which are only temporary, are eliminated in moments of vision in which the hero suddenly perceives a unity of the internal and external worlds. The tone of such fictions is usually optimistic.

Miss Lonelyhearts is obviously not of this type. It is more firmly one of the second variety of novels of psychological development, one we might call the "existential," the "chaotic experience," or the anti-romance novel. Here isolation is a permanent condition; the progress of the psyche, if there is any, is toward more intensive isolation, perhaps death. The tone of such works is ironic. Moments occur which might have become revelatory but which fail to transform the protagonist or resolve his problems. Consequently the protagonist is never able to achieve the object of his search, the ability to act. He is immobilized. The search becomes a wait. This kind of progression characterizes *Miss Lonelyhearts*. The fixed moral and psychological dilemma of man is morbidly attractive; his search for answers is necessary but futile. We are given the situation and expectation pattern of the "artist as young man" type, but they are used ironically.

II

After the publication of *Miss Lonelyhearts* West wrote a piece on his novelistic technique. In it he said, "The novelist is no longer a psychologist. Psychology can become much more important. The great body of case histories can be used in the way the ancient writers used their myths. Freud is your Bulfinch; you can learn from him." Psychologists have articulated for the novelist the archetypal dramas of human existence; the novelist may then use these "stories" as he wishes, freed of the necessity to observe the minutiae of the psychic life. West uses Freud in this way in *Miss Lonelyhearts*. The focal character is portrayed as a neurotic through whose psychic conflict the dimensions of man's condition can be measured. The details of his neurosis are given occasionally, but only to create a feeling of internal verisimilitude or to introduce a metaphor of structural importance. This is not a novel of psychological realism.

The central figure, Miss Lonelyhearts, finds himself in a neurotic state because he cannot effect a compromise between a life of reason and a life of feeling. He sees suffering all about him, and he sees this as evidence of chaos. Under the cloud of irreconcilable conflict and intuitions of chaos, he is driven into an escape world, the world of euphoric experience. Even there his tensions assert themselves, but in symbolic terms. But in his dreams or visions he finds solutions, resolutions, which he cannot find in the course of external life.

The psychoanalyst Wilhelm Stekel described this neurotic retreat in a metaphor which West himself uses throughout the book: "The polyphony of thought draws its energy out of the organs. In the [neurotic], the psychic and physical equilibrium is disturbed. Disharmonies make life unbearable for him. He belongs more to dreams than reality. He hearkens to the middle voices." This is certainly an accurate description of the pattern of Miss Lonelyhearts's experience. Whenever he encounters a difficult interpersonal problem which demands a solution dictated by him, he retreats to the noisy isolation of the speakeasy or to the impregnable fortress of his bed. Eventually, even his bed-hideaway is discovered, and he finds that he must erect a wall around himself so that the outside world cannot assault him with its spoon-fed soup and its easy advice. He becomes a "rock" impervious to the incursion of the "sea." ("What goes on in the sea is of no interest to the rock.")

But Miss L's neurotic state is the center of a universe which is immobilized by this internal conflict. As one of the faceless-drinkers in the speakeasy observes, while commenting on Miss L's dilemma, "The trouble with him, the trouble with all of us, is that we have no outer life, only an inner one, and that by necessity." Miss L's sickness, the progress of the retreat from life because of anxiety, provides West with the superstructure of his novel; texturing materials are the metaphors and images which arise from the music of the "middle voices," the euphoric escape experiences of his anti-hero.

The pathos of Miss Lonelyhearts's condition is that he knows that he is sick, but he finds that he can do nothing about it. He does not always retreat from the situation. Though he cannot actively find an answer to his problem, he does allow himself to be preached at, spoon-fed, led by the hand to the speakeasy, the country, the bed; he seems to hope that someone will show him the way. The dominant dramatic pattern of the work is an alternation between encounters with life in which someone else tries to show him a program for the solution of his problems and a retreat into himself in which the problem is worked out in his unconscious.

Miss L recognizes that the basis of his malaise is his inability to fuse feeling and sense into an attitude or an effective program of action. In internal terms he cannot harmonize the dictates of head with those of heart. He cannot abstract himself from his feelings and thus go about acting on them. He is pulled apart by these polarities and has only intuitions of order in the midst of chaos. This order-chaos problem exists in the external world as well, for the adversity with which he is in constant contact exists as an element of the forces of destruction and dissolution. Naturally, not being able to solve his internal problems, he cannot begin to give advice to others on solving their external ones. Thus adversity, pictured so dramatically in the letters he receives, only activates his own internal disorder. The correspondence helps him to externalize his problem, but then his inability to assist only further frustrates him. Failing to help in any way, he becomes incapable of action on any level of his life. Chaos reigns.

In characteristically neurotic fashion, he fights chaos by developing an "insane sensitiveness to order." He looks to those who appear to have ordered lives, and he offers to let one or another lead him. Each time, he finally recognizes that all order is only transitory. In the depth of one of his "fevers" he sees clearly that chaos is part of the very essence of the external world and that order must come from within to be even momentarily effective. He phantasizes that he is in the midst of a pawnshop window, viewing "the paraphernalia of suffering," the furniture of chaos. He comes to realize that

> man has a tropism for order. Keys in one pocket, change in another. Mandolins are tuned GDAE. The physical world has a tropism for disorder, entropy. Man against nature . . . the battle of the centuries. Keys yearn to mix with change. Mandolins strive to get out of tune. Every order has within it the germs of destruction.

Thus he projects his problem in terms of a cosmic dialectic, recognizing that to be human and sane he must find a rational organizing principle.

But the order he searches for is not one of things, but of experience which will enable him to guide future action. He needs a program of action which will synthesize the dictates of heart and head. The conventionally accepted systems of order he is offered he finds unacceptable, incomplete, and inconsistent with these inner needs. But he can't find an answer within himself either.

The result is an inability to act, think, even write the letters demanded by his job. He is immobilized and muted. When he tries to talk, he finds that "his tongue . . . [has] become a fat thumb." His only release from the tensions created by the need to communicate and the inability to do so is in sadistic action, retreat into self, or a passive resignation to the wishes of others.

Consequently, when he does act, it is not in line with any program but simply in blind *re*action. Actions become only twitch-rejections, nothing more. He wants to have a purpose, to advance into life, but because of his lack of confidence and self-control he retreats from others, becoming submerged periodically in the fevered world of his own making. He engages with another only when the other takes the initiative. "Like a dead man, only friction could make him warm or violence make him mobile." He occasionally has life rubbed into him, but each time his inner conflicts force him to turn on those who have forced him out of his cell. This rejection adds to the depth of the defeat, deepening his sense of chaos, loss of control, and isolation.

This pattern of rejection is felt very strongly by Miss L because it represents a failure of heart. His heart dictates acceptance, not rejection. It is only in his fantasy world that this acceptance principle ever seems to be effected, and at those few moments internal harmony is achieved.

III

Miss Lonelyhearts's rejection of the life-programs which are offered to him by others occurs because each lacks this ability to harmonize through acceptance. The two attitudes most persistently injected into Miss L's life are those of cynicism and optimistic sentimentalism. The cynic interprets the world as corrupt and would ignore or cast doubt on all evidence to the contrary. To protect himself against the incursions of this corruption he erects a barrier of reasoned noninvolvement in which control of life is achieved through the recognition of its dominant pattern and the development of psychic detachment. The sentimentalist on the other hand sees life as purposive and good. He would ignore evil or inequity and construct a world in which only goodness and beauty and happiness would find place. Both, then, would arbitrarily limit experience, one in favor of the head; the other, the heart.

In allegorical fashion one character represents monistically each of these points of view. Shrike is the complete cynic; Betty, the total pastoral sentimentalist. Both argue as prophets of "the true way" in an attempt to convince Miss L. But Miss L recognizes the restrictive quality of both points of view in their tendency to forget important areas of life. Miss L says this of Betty: "Her world was not the world and could never include the readers of his column. Her sureness was based on the power to limit experience arbitrarily." The same could be said of Shrike, but Miss L never takes him seriously enough to comment on his cynical approach. Though Miss L is confused, and they do not seem to be, his "confusion was significant, while [their] order was not." Both Shrike and Betty would ignore suffering, accepting arbitrary order as truth. The order for which Miss L searches must come from inclusiveness and total acceptance, not exclusiveness and rejection. It must be a unity of disparate parts.

Shrike and Betty are the two most important people in the life of Miss L. They are the ones who most frequently rub him into life. Both see that he is wracked by confusion and indecision and see this as a sign of innocence, naiveté, and immaturity. Each talks to him as if he were a child, Shrike speaking as if he were his father, Betty, his mother. Both want him to become a man, though they differ radically on what such a step would mean. Ultimately, Miss L's rejection of them and their points of view occurs because he recognizes that theirs are worlds of their own creation, childish fantasy worlds. They, not he, are the ones in need of growing up.

Furthermore, each is not what he seems to be. Shrike likes to portray himself in paternal terms, as a phallically superior male, one with control and authority. His control is too reliant on his rapier-sharp handling of words; in actions he is a failure. Ultimately he is unmasked as feckless and impotent — his phallicism only degenerate sadism. With his own wife, sex is impossible; with the ever available, faceless Rose Farkis, his caresses are dispassionate and calculated, his kiss, the burying of his "triangular face like the blade of a hatchet in her neck."

Betty imagines herself a country maiden, an earth-mother, a symbol of fecundity. However, it soon becomes evident that she has anesthetized herself to the sensual side of life. Not even Miss L's sadistic pluck at her roselike nipple can stir her. The profundities of birth or death mean nothing to her. Though seduced and pregnant at the end of the story, she continues to think and act like a virgin. Her fecund sexuality resolves itself into little more than a casual masochism. She is not like any animal of the fields, easily available in the matter of increase; rather, she is "like a kitten whose soft helplessness makes one ache to hurt it."

Betty and Shrike are paired against each other vying for Miss L's allegiance throughout this work, and their images are projected in contrasting terms. Not only are the male-female, paternal-maternal, sadism-masochism dichotomies employed in defining their roles, but also the split between city and country. Shrike is the man of the city with all the attendant traits of world-weariness and sophistication, while Betty is the innocent country girl without wile.

The city reflects the most vicious and sadistic, the most defeated aspects of life. The most recurrent symbol of this attitude is the little park which

Miss L sits in or walks through so often. It is first described in the most agonizing terms:

> He entered the park at the North Gate and swallowed mouthfuls of the heavy shade that curtained its arch. He walked into the shadow of a lamp-post that lay on the path like a spear. It pierced him like a spear.
>
> As far as he could discover, there were no signs of spring. The decay that covered the surface of the mottled ground was not the kind in which life generates. Last year, he remembered, May had failed to quicken these soiled fields. It had taken all the brutality of July to torture a few green spikes through the exhausted dirt.

This wasteland is as theatrically and sadistically castratory as Shrike. In one description the same defeated sexuality becomes even more pronounced, for the park comes to life and is exhibitionistically autoerotic.

> When he reached the little park he slumped down on a bench opposite the Mexican War obelisk.
>
> The stone shaft cast a long, rigid shadow on the walk in front of him. He sat staring at it without knowing why until he noticed that it was lengthening in rapid jerks, not as shadows usually lengthen. He grew frightened and looked up quickly at the monument. It seemed red and swollen in the dying sun, as though it were about to spout a load of granite seed.

Betty argues true country values and finally persuades Miss L to visit a farm owned by her aunt. In the country the sodden fruitless valley of the city springs into perspective, and he is partially revived and duped by the country air, the owls, the loons, and the deer. He is even able to eat an apple with Betty and take a fall with her on the earth, ignoring his perception that the life-process was little better off in the country than in the city: ". . . they went for a walk in the woods. It was very sad under the trees. Although spring was well advanced, in the deep shade there was nothing but death—rotten leaves, gray and white fungi, and over everything a funereal hush." Both worlds are tainted with the smells of decay and death at the very times when life should be asserting itself. But the country world seems to be calmly accepting this condition, while the city is actively proselytizing for it. Miss L really only wants "to cultivate his interior garden" anyway. The two worlds reflect the values of their defenders. Betty sees the corruption of the city; Shrike, the "dull" quality of the country; but neither can see the sterility of their own worlds.

Betty, for all her country ideals, is really nothing but the great American housewife. Her order is based on social decorum, the straightening of the tie or the wearing of the gingham apron, not on the primal course of the cycle of nature. She can't stand smells, especially human ones, and that is her real reason for rejecting the city. The suburbs would really fill the bill.

In her own way Betty is an avatar of the girl next door, the sentimental one who feels a fateful quality in her loving, but who never really loves. Her sentimental approach has her submerged in feeling, but experiencing no passion, "all heart and no genitals." To be sure, she "gives herself" to Miss L, but not through any primal attraction. Rather, she wants to save him, redeem him, and order his life by putting his slippers by the crackling fire so that he'll be comfortable when he comes home at night. She firmly accepts the American belief that women are the center of the moral universe, placed on earth to bring order to men. Any man is redeemable so long as the right woman comes along. Miss L rejects her and her world twice, not with guilt, but with annoyance "at having been fooled into thinking that such a solution was possible." In his final mood of acceptance he does say that he will marry her since she is pregnant, but by then he has become the impervious rock in such a state of mind that nothing can disturb him.

If Betty is "all heart and no genitals," Shrike is all head and false genitals. He is the vilifier of Greek comedy, carrying with him his bludgeon; or he is the court fool, exuding wit and badinage, carrying his false staff by which he parodies the king. But strangely, he takes himself seriously, acting as though his authority were real, speaking as if he represented truth. Fortunately, Miss L accepts Shrike's verbiage as trivial, his authority as assailable. Shrike never becomes more than a lord of misrule, an agent of chaos in a world turned upside down.

One of Shrike's favorite roles is that of anti-Christ devil. His name, beyond referring to the sadistic bird who impales his prey on thorns, is almost an anagram on the name of Christ. He is the man who sees himself as the bearer of the word, but his cynicism and basically destructive nature reveal him to be the false Messiah. His position as anti-Christ is made evident in the first lines of the book where he parodies the litany *anima christi* in the manner of the Black Mass, a calumny that reoccurs in other forms throughout the book.

> Soul of Miss L, glorify me.
> Body of Miss L, nourish me.
> Blood of Miss L, intoxicate me.
> Tears of Miss L, wash me.

He articulates the "Gospel according to Shrike" and posits a new style trinity composed of "Father, Son and Wirehaired Fox Terrier."

Shrike's badinage is mere show; when confronted in his home, he admits to inabilities with his wife, blaming her, of course. He claims that "sleeping with her is like sleeping with a knife in one's groin." This is probably true. From what we know of Mary, she is the perfect mate for Shrike. She, too, is dispassionate, frigid, a tease who talks freely but who is incapable of action. Everything about her is sadistically calculated to attract and frustrate men. If Shrike is a parody Messiah, she is a travesty of the Virgin, eternal symbol of miraculous fecundity. She allows Miss L to rub against her, even to undress her in the hall, but never to have coitus with her. Her manner of dress is a perfect reflection of her painful seductiveness: "She was wearing a tight, shiny dress that was like glass-covered steel and there was something cleanly mechanical in her pantomime." She is as dehumanized and insensate as her husband.

Though Mary and Betty are opposed in most respects, they share sexual anesthesia. Each leaves Miss L feeling unfulfilled and empty because of their easy limitation of experience. Fay Doyle represents a further incomplete mode of life. She has neither head nor heart, only a body and a physical drive which she inflicts on the docile Miss L. She is totally primal, and her drive is given in cosmic terms. Her breath is "sea sounds," her call, a "sea-moan," her rhythm of life, "moon-driven." Even her way of speaking is hypnotic and incantatory in its "tom-tom" rhythm. Her speech shows a failure of both heart and head in its lack of common sense or logic and its revelation of casual bigotry. After her initial seduction of Miss L, in which he willingly reverses roles with her, she, too, is rejected because of her limited approach to life.

Her husband, Peter Doyle, mirrors the deepest of Miss L's problems. He, too, is a real lonelyheart, crippled by life, needing love so badly that he is willing to go to ridiculous extremes to get it. Whereas Miss L is an emotional cripple, Peter is physically deformed. Fay Doyle causes both of them to assume the passive role, Peter going even farther than Miss L, once becoming a lap dog. Both are muted by their infirmities, Peter perhaps more completely so.

> When the cripple finally labored into speech, Miss Lonelyhearts was unable to understand him. He listened hard for a few minutes and realized that Doyle was making no attempt to be understood. He was giving birth to groups of words that lived inside of him as things, a jumble of retorts he had meant to make when insulted and the private curses against fate that experience had taught him to swallow.

Miss L recognizes the bond between himself and Peter and in so doing feels a sudden strength and compassion. In a real act of love he takes Peter by the hand while sitting in the speakeasy and tries to convey through his continued touch the depth of his understanding and love. Peter never understands, however, and eventually becomes the instrument of Miss L's death.

IV

It is the vision of the possibility of love as a unifying force which provides Miss L with his ability to persist throughout the work. He associates love with Christ and at certain important times tries to make himself over in Christ's image. He says to Betty, "I've got a Christ complex . . . Humanity . . . I'm a humanity lover." This means a number of things in this book. At times it seems to imply that he sees himself as the impaled Christ, the Man of Sorrows dying for the sins of the world. More often, however, it is Christ as unifier, Christ as Saviour, Prince of Love, that dominates, but this is when unity visits him in his vision, not when he goes out to capture control of life. In his own room he lives like a priest, and it is there that Christian deliverance occurs through meditation on the figure of the crucified Saviour. But when he tries to become a priest in the outside world, with his correspondents or with Peter and Fay Doyle, he becomes mute and ineffective. Love may work when it dictates to the individual, but as the basis for a program of interaction it is doomed, this parable seems to tell us.

But the principle of Love is the only one that Miss L can accept, because it is the only one which takes into account all of the contradictory forces of human experience and gives them order. Two interrelated problems which Miss L learns to cope with through love are violence and sexuality.

The vocabulary of violence dominates this novel. From the letters to the newspaper at the beginning, to the final, meaningless shooting at the end, the work expresses its deepest intuitions of chaotic life in terms of destruction. Miss L feels this violence strongly, but he has learned to cope with it neither in the outside world nor in his own nature. He recognizes that violence as destruction is akin to chaos; while it exists, attempts at order are doomed.

Surely the reason why the letters describing adversity affect him so deeply is that he himself is capable of blindly destroying and thus causing adversity in the lives of others. But he is also capable of feeling deep guilt at the expression of his impulsive destruction, and he consequently places himself in a position where *he* will be hurt. This alternation of attitudes is the sadomasochistic pattern, and it accounts for an important inner rhythm in the structure of this novel.

The work begins with the first of Shrike's savage onslaughts. This, combined with the effect of the unfathomable distress of his correspondents on his mood, seems to send Miss L into a state of savage depression. Following this are three scenes in which Miss L commences an act of love only to experience failure which causes the action to turn into sadistic violence. The first is a flashback. He is reminded of a youthful experience, of a time when he and some friends went to the woods to sacrifice a lamb. The ceremony soon deteriorated, for the knife they used broke, and they left the animal there bleeding to death. Later, Miss L returned and savagely kicked the rest of the life out of the lamb.

The next scene replays the sadistic destructive action on an innocent creature. Miss L goes to see Betty, whom he hasn't visited in two months, since they had first become engaged. His heart has failed him, and he calls up the instinct to hurt others in reprisal for his feeling of inner void. He treats her in a brutal fashion, assailing her both physically and mentally and leaves her in tears.

This scene is followed by another reminiscence—this time of two mass rapes of women, told in heartless terms. Then there is the most violent and sadistic scene of the work, once again illustrative of Miss L's basic pattern of the frustration of initial love impulse. After getting punched for being polite during a drinking spree in his speakeasy, Miss L and a friend go walking. In the wasteland park they spy a "clean, old man" in the comfort station. The man is the perfect outgrowth of this park, a harmless, feckless, castrato who mirrors many of Miss L's own failures and inabilities. They take pity on this man and invite him to have a drink, which he accepts. Then the two begin to give the man the third degree, and the performance becomes increasingly merciless. The grotesque man becomes mute with fright. Finally, Miss L insanely begins to twist the man's arm.

After this orgy of sadistic action, Miss L seems to undergo feelings of remorse. He immediately places himself in a position where he must be used, hurt, vilified. He invites Mary Shrike out, knowing that she will tease and then refuse him. Then he allows himself to be seduced by Fay Doyle. Thoroughly beaten, he retreats to his bed and to fevered visions of harmony in diversity. In such a state, Betty is able to persuade him to go to the farm, and the cycle begins once more, although not at such a violent level.

These sadistic and masochistic expressions are a reflection of Miss L's inner fears and emerge as demonstrations of hate. Hate is the drive to power and arises from a context of lack of control. Love is the ability to renounce hate and power and the will to submit to the demands of a higher organizing force (such as the family system, society, and God). This submission is totally different from that of masochism, for rather than being the expression of a will to control (in masochism, deflected from the external world back onto self destructively because of guilt), it is the renunciation of power. Not too strangely, Miss L finds that in the world of Shrike and Betty he cannot feel and act on love. They activate only those parts of his inner life which he fears, hates, and reacts against. Little wonder, then, that he retreats into himself and his cell of solitude when confronted by the demands of that life.

This problem with violence is closely related to Miss L's problems of sexual identity. Social norm dictates that a man is active in all realms of life, especially his relations with women. Similarly, men are supposed to act through the dictates of reason, by using their heads. This is the model of manliness which Shrike pretends to portray, and he very explicitly demands that Miss L emulate him in this respect. But by so demanding, Shrike creates a basic confusion in his relation with Miss L. He speaks from the vantage of authority and greater experience, treating Miss L as if he were a child. Thus, while demanding emulation, he is also insisting upon passive obedience. Shrike's role as authority figure and proposed ego-ideal, therefore, creates an initial conflict which is further complicated by the revelation that Shrike is not the superior male he pretends to be.

Betty, too, tries to reshape Miss L's world to conform to her values. She seems to argue that tidiness is of utmost importance, even if it involves retreat and docility in the face of adverse reality on both of their parts. If he will become the rightful provider, she will keep his bungalow world clean and orderly. But she, too, has an internal inconsistency in her approach, for though she preaches the sentimental-masochistic approach to life, her assailable position only brings out the sadistic side of Miss L's nature, thus making him more of a man in Shrike's mold.

Both Betty's and Shrike's images of manliness are sexless, however. Both demand a renunciation of the true coming together of the sexes in a love state for something much less. Only Fay allows him a truly sexual expression, but it is a totally infantile one—she makes of him a baby, forcing his head to her breast. This is closer to his ideal; he does find momentary pleasure in having her reverse the usual roles.

The sadomasochistic cycle is one of three parts: sadistic action, masochistic docility, and retreat to bed and isolation. This tripartite arrangement is also true of the available routes of sexual expression. One may become active and male, passive and female, or regressive and infantile. "The human being does not consist of man and woman, but of man, woman, and child." Each of these components has attributes which are vital in the balance of human experience. Man is capable of abstract thought and of action on principle; woman, of feeling and intuitive sympathy; child, of living and acting in the context of beautiful innocence.

The shock of adverse experience provides Miss L and the others with their greatest problem and defines for them their approaches to life. The monism of each of the subsidiary characters is determined in part by his handling of some shock provided by rejection or some other adverse experience. Both Mary and Shrike are immobilized and desensitized by their confrontations with the fullness and duplicity of life. Mary punctuates her teasing rejection of Miss L by reminiscing about her mother's rejection of her through death from breast cancer—all this while allowing herself to be undressed. Shrike, somehow emasculated by experience in the past, allows this trauma to be constantly re-enacted by marrying frigid Mary. Fay, betrayed sexually, spends the rest of her life getting back at men by marrying Peter, a man she can hurt repeatedly. Peter, rejected by life in his disability, tries to acquire a protecting mother by marrying the already pregnant Fay, only to have her emphasize his impotence by her rude treatment of him and by her infidelities. Each chooses to re-enact traumatic experience in his own fixed pattern, some identifying with the mechanism of rejection and acting on it, the others, acquiescing, constantly replaying the initial experience of defeat.

Betty alone is not defeated by experience, and this is why she can assert more influence on Miss L. Her life pattern is determined by a rejection of experience and a permanent prolongation of the state of innocence. Her vision of perfection is, not surprisingly, the country world. In this she invokes a persistent American solution to the problem of the experience of life in society—retreat to the woods where one's self-sufficiency will assert itself under the ordering eye of Mother Nature. Her answer to the duality of head and heart is to regress to the childlike state of mind in which the potential of reasoned judgment has not yet arisen. Her resolution for the dichotomy of the sexes is to retreat to that period when such differences had not yet asserted themselves, that state in which each person was individually and narcissistically self-sufficient. This sexual wish-state is that of androgyny— everyone a hermaphrodite, a perfect balance of sexes. Such androgynes need no others to experience fulfillment; they are able to exist in a state of permanent innocence and self-sufficiency.

This androgynous state is greatly desired by Miss L, but he must reject Betty's way of achieving it because of her retreat from life. He wants to advance into existence, accepting the dualities of life and finding a unity in diversity. Retreat from the unpleasant side of things, or rejection of it, smacks of self-love and self-defeat; his answer must be selfless.

In visions he finds this solution in Christ and the doctrine of *agape,* the selfless love of acceptance. In Christ he finds not a retreat from life to former innocence, but rather a reinstatement of innocence on Man by Christ's redemptive presence. He feels in the power of Jesus the enforcement of harmony in the midst of diversity — the making of life into a whole of conflicting parts by the acceptance of order in divinity. It is the vision of Jesus given in Galatians: "There is neither Jew nor Greek, there is neither bond nor free, there is neither male nor female; for ye are all one in Christ Jesus." The harmonization of discordant forces, the reinstatement of androgynous innocence, occurs not in the deceptive simplicity of any verdant Eden, but on barren Calvary hill.

In the transport of a "fever" in the solitude of his room after administering the Eucharist to himself with crackers and water Jesus comes alive as Miss L stares at his impaled figure. Jesus becomes a bright fly, the world, a leaping fish which consumes the fly and is ennobled by it by exuding a bright beauty and a splash of music. All else in the room seems dead next to this image; Christ becomes the totality of "life and light." At this point head and heart and innocence and fruition all come together: "He felt clean and fresh. His heart was a rose and in his skull another rose bloomed."

The roses are the result of his cultivation of the "garden of his mind," and he has become the new Androgynes in the garden-state. He is able to formulate a plan of action based on his new acceptance of divine order, in which all of his columns will be submitted to God. But the vision is a fleeting one. He is immediately confronted with his other self, crippled Peter, who has come to kill him. In his first gesture of love under this new plan, he goes to embrace Peter, is misunderstood, and is accidentally shot. As someone has observed earlier in the book, it is very difficult "to find a market for the fruits of . . . personality," for the flowers of even the most effectively cultivated "interior garden." The response to an act of love is the same as that to any other stimulus, absurd destruction and death.

Religious Experience in *Miss Lonelyhearts*

Marcus Smith

The main critical issue concerning *Miss Lonelyhearts* is whether the title character and protagonist is a tragic saint or a psychotic fool. James Light, for example, champions the "saint" school by arguing that Miss Lonelyhearts is profoundly concerned with the search for "some spiritual reality to believe in and live by," a quest that ends in "tragic disillusionment":

> Miss Lonelyhearts, wishing to succor with love all the desperate of the universe and expecting to perform a miracle by which the cripple will be cured, runs rapturously toward Doyle. But there is no miracle. Instead Miss Lonelyhearts is shot by Doyle, destroyed, like Christ, by the panic and ignorance of those whom he would save. Doyle, and in him suffering man, shatters the only solution to the intolerableness of man's pain, destroys the Christlike man who perceives that love and faith are the only answers to man's pain in a universe he cannot understand.

The opposite view is represented by Arthur Cohen, who, in a *Commonweal* review of *The Complete Works of Nathanael West,* says that Miss Lonelyhearts's "Christ complex" is "precisely a complex, not a belief in specific documents of faith, not faith in any order of sacrament or scheme of salvation. It is a complex, a fixation of the mind." Miss Lonelyhearts, in Cohen's final evaluation, "misrepresents the world and is martyr to his misrepresentation."

These contrary positions are not easily resolved. However, an extremely important clue is West's "Some Notes on *Miss Lonelyhearts,*" published

From *Contemporary Literature* 9, no. 2 (Spring 1968). © 1968 by the Regents of the University of Wisconsin.

shortly after the novel. These "Notes," though brief and fragmented, tell us what West thought of his title character and name two key sources:

> Miss Lonelyhearts became the portrait of a priest of our time who has a religious experience. His case is classical and is built on all the cases in James' *Varieties of Religious Experience* and Starbuck's *Psychology of Religion*. The psychology is theirs not mine. The immagery [sic] is mine. Chapt. I — maladjustment. Chapter III — the need for taking symbols literally is described through a dream in which a symbol is actually fleshed. Chapter IV — deadness and disorder, see Lives of Bunyan and Tolstoy. Chapter VI — self-torture by conscious sinning: see life of any saint. And so on.

This passage demonstrates, I think, that West did not view his protagonist as either a saint or a psychotic; instead, he suggests that these two categories, in the twentieth century at least, far from being exclusive of each other, are perhaps identical. On the one hand Miss Lonelyhearts is "a priest of our time," and at the same time he suffers from "maladjustment . . . deadness and disorder . . . self-torture by conscious sinning. . . ." West, therefore, did not consider the saintly madman (or the lunatic saint) an impossible figure. Furthermore, this view is supported and the role of West's protagonist clarified when we turn to West's acknowledged sources, William James and Edwin Diller Starbuck. For these philosophers, religious experience often contains irrational, subjective, and even psychotic elements, and the "psychology" of Miss Lonelyhearts is, indeed, theirs.

James's *Varieties of Religious Experience* is by far the more important of the two sources, even though West indicates no priority. Starbuck's *Psychology of Religion* is the earlier work and is limited to a statistical study of religious conversion, mainly during adolescence, and chiefly among American Protestants. James's *Varieties,* originating as the Gifford Lectures on Natural Religion delivered at Edinburgh in 1901–1902, drew on Starbuck but ranged more widely and deeply into the philosophical as well as psychological significance of religious experience, before, during, and after conversion. Starbuck cannot, however, be ignored. Very often he and James describe the same or similar religious experience or psychological type. James's "Sick Soul," for example, corresponds roughly to Starbuck's period of "storm and stress," and the former's "Twice born soul" is analogous to the latter's "new life." Nevertheless, James is the more important of the two acknowledged sources and his "varieties" clarifies several of the characters in *Miss Lonelyhearts.*

West said the subject of the opening chapter of *Miss Lonelyhearts* was "maladjustment," and he is right if he means that Miss Lonelyhearts is unable to cope with either the large or the minute aspects of reality. The novel opens with his staring at Shrike's mocking prayer:

> Although the deadline was less than a quarter of an hour away, he was still working on his leader. He had gone as far as: "Life *is* worth while, for it is full of dreams and peace, gentleness and ecstasy, and faith that burns like a clear white flame on a grim dark altar." But he found it impossible to continue. The letters were no longer funny. He could not go on finding the same joke funny thirty times a day for months on end. And on most days he received more than thirty letters, all of them alike, stamped from the dough of suffering with a heart-shaped cookie knife.

Miss Lonelyhearts's "maladjustment" coincides in several important ways with the religious variety James calls the Sick Soul. The Sick Soul is obsessed with the presence and force of evil, and is convinced that "the evil aspects of our life are of its very essence," and that "the world's meaning most comes home to us when we lay them [the evil aspects] most to heart." Moreover, there are "shallower and profounder levels" of the Sick Soul phenomenon: "There are people for whom evil means only a maladjustment with *things,* a wrong correspondence of one's life with the environment." This Sick Soul can be cured "by modifying either the self or the things, or both at once." But, says James, "there are others for whom evil is no mere relation of the subject to particular outer things, but something more radical and general, a wrongness or vice in his essential nature, which no alteration of the environment, or any superficial rearrangement of the inner self, can cure, and which requires a supernatural remedy."

Miss Lonelyhearts, considered as a Sick Soul, seems to partake of both the "shallower and profounder levels." The environmental conflict is implicitly present through most of the novel. But Miss Lonelyhearts in the early parts of the novel is primarily an example of the "profounder" Sick Soul, "which no alteration of the environment, or any superficial rearrangement of the inner self, can cure."

In his "Notes" West refers to Bunyan and Tolstoy, and it is in his lecture on the Sick Soul that James first uses the example of Tolstoy, whose melancholia he characterized as anhedonia; that is, the "passive loss of appetite for all life's values":

> In Tolstoy's case the sense that life had any meaning whatever was for a time wholly withdrawn. The result was a transformation in the whole expression of reality. When we come to study

the phenomenon of conversion or religious regeneration, we shall see that a not infrequent consequence of the change operated in the subject is a transfiguration of the face of nature in his eyes. A new heaven seems to shine upon a new earth. In melancholiacs there is usually a similar change, only it is in the reverse direction. The world now looks remote, strange, sinister, uncanny. Its color is gone, its breath is cold.

Miss Lonelyhearts's view of the world is remarkably similar in the early part of the novel. In the second chapter, as he is walking to Delehanty's speakeasy, he crosses a small park:

As far as he could discover, there were no signs of spring. The decay that covered the surface of the mottled ground was not the kind in which life generates. Last year, he remembered, May had failed to quicken these soiled fields. It had taken all the brutality of July to torture a few green spikes through the exhausted dirt.

The response here (echoing Eliot's *Waste Land* in its sterile imagery) marks Miss Lonelyhearts as a clear example of anhedonia. And James emphasizes that anhedonia is a subjective state of perception. In other words, the outer world is changed by the inner disturbance. Notice that West opens with, "*As far as he could discover,* there were no signs of spring," thereby signifying that within his objective omniscient frame, West is shifting to the morbid anhedonic point of view of Miss Lonelyhearts. On the next page, the same thing occurs: "*He searched the sky for a target.* But the gray sky looked as if it had been rubbed with a soiled eraser." Throughout the novel, West uses this biased point of view, in which the freedom of the omniscient method is combined with the subjective immediacy of his character's perceptions and responses.

James discusses the Sick Soul's quest for a "supernatural remedy." To the Sick Soul, "the happiness of Eden never comes again." Instead, when happiness does come to this type, it is "not the simple ignorance of ill, but something vastly more complex. . . . The process is one of redemption, not of mere reversion to natural health, and the sufferer, when saved, is saved by what seems to him a second birth, a deeper kind of conscious being than he could enjoy before."

The subject of "a second birth" and its relationship to *Miss Lonelyhearts* is important and I will return to it. What I want to discuss now is the relationship between Miss Lonelyhearts and Betty. In contrast to the Sick Soul, Healthy-Mindedness is what James calls the "once-born" consciousness, which develops "straight and natural, with no element of morbid compunction or crisis." The "once-born" personality is psychologically the reciprocal of the Sick Soul. Where the Sick Soul is morbid, filled with and overpowered by the sense of evil in the world, the Healthy-Minded person is cheerful and, in his optimistic outlook, unable even to comprehend evil. As in the case of the Sick Soul, James distinguishes between varieties of Healthy-Mindedness:

> In its involuntary variety, healthy-mindedness is a way of feeling happy about things immediately. In its systematical variety, it is an abstract way of conceiving things as good. . . . Systematic healthy-mindedness, conceiving good as the essential and univer- sal aspect of being, deliberately excludes evil from its field of vision.

Turning to West's novel, we find at the heart of the relationship be- tween Miss Lonelyhearts and Betty the conflict between his morbidity and her systematic optimism. Betty stands for order, simplicity, childish innocence. Miss Lonelyhearts "had once thought that if her world were larger, were *the* world, she might order it as finally as the objects on her dressing table." But he knows that "Her world was not the world and could never include the readers of his column. Her sureness was based on the power to limit experience arbitrarily." When Miss Lonelyhearts visits Betty in the fourth chapter, and after he has viciously grabbed her breast, Betty's reaction is only to ask, "Are you sick?" This infuriates Miss Lonelyhearts. He shouts at her: "What a kind bitch you are. As soon as anyone acts viciously, you say he's sick. Wife-torturers, rapers of small children, according to you they're all sick. No morality, only medicine."

James says antagonisms "may naturally arise" between the Sick Soul and the Healthy-Minded, because to "the morbid-minded way . . . healthy- mindedness pure and simple seems unspeakably blind and shallow. To the healthy-minded way . . . the way of the sick-soul seems unmanly and diseased." This is an extremely accurate description of the conflict between Betty and Miss Lonelyhearts in the first part of the novel. Thus, Betty insists that Miss Lonelyhearts is sick and in need of her care. He replies that she is limited and shallow, that she cannot clearly comprehend (as he can) the evil and suf- fering in the world. Later, when Miss Lonelyhearts has been in his room for two days in a state of collapse, Betty visits him ("I heard you were sick"), feeds him hot soup, and puts his room in order. She tries to convince him that he should quit the Miss Lonelyhearts job, or, in other words, arbitrarily divert his attention from disease and death and thereby become well. Betty's healthy-minded "weapon for self-protection against disturbance" offers itself to Miss Lonelyhearts. And his response is precisely that of the Jamesian Sick Soul: "You don't understand, Betty, I can't quit. And even if I were to quit, it wouldn't make any difference. I wouldn't be able to forget the letters, no matter what I did." The reason it would make no difference is, as James puts it, "morbid-mindedness ranges over a wider scale of experience" than healthy-mindedness. Miss Lonelyhearts is psychologically unable to "limit experience arbitrarily," which is what Betty does to preserve her healthy-mindedness.

Furthermore, James, while describing both states as distorted, clearly sympathizes more with the Sick Soul than with the Healthy-Minded. One reason is the lack of tolerance in the latter: "If religious intolerance and hanging and burning could again become the order of the day . . . the healthy-minded would . . . show themselves the less indulgent party of the two." But the main reason James rejects Healthy-Mindedness is that "the evil facts which it refuses positively to account for are a genuine portion of reality; and they may after all be the best key to life's significance, and possibly the only openers of our eyes to the deepest levels of truth."

A parallel distinction is implicit in *Miss Lonelyhearts*. While West obviously develops Miss Lonelyhearts as a Sick Soul, Betty's Healthy-Mindedness is not a viable alternative. She *does* offer Miss Lonelyhearts a way out, an escape from the ugly world of the letters into the bland world of an advertising agency, a wife, children, gingham curtains and a picket fence; but this alternative demands that Miss Lonelyhearts, like Betty, "limit experience arbitrarily." He cannot do so, and therefore he grows into an insane saintliness. This is, paradoxically, a psychological growth, a movement into a broader though destructive level of experience.

In the "process of redemption" Miss Lonelyhearts's Sick Soul goes through several stages, and in a number of ways conforms to the process of religious conversion as described by James and Starbuck. In the opening of the book, as we have seen, Miss Lonelyhearts, though sick, is a deliberate nonbeliever. Through the seventh chapter ("Miss Lonelyhearts on a field trip") we see him groping desperately for some tangible, secular escape from his morbid awareness of the world's evil. He tries liquor (chapters 2 and 5), semi-philosophic reading — *The Brothers Karamazov* (chapter 3), Betty (chapter 4), violence (chapter 5), sex (chapters 4, 6, and 7) — and nothing helps much, for in chapter eight, after Mrs. Doyle has left him, "Miss Lonelyhearts became physically sick and was unable to leave his room." This is the first crisis, the first breakdown. But it also is the beginning of his redemption or rebirth, for when he awakes from his hallucinatory dream in which he makes "a gigantic cross," he is "weak, yet calm." The stability of his consciousness, though temporary, is the first stage in his development towards a second birth.

James has much to say about the redemptive process in his lecture, "The

Divided Self, and the Process of its Unification." First, for the Sick Soul, "Peace cannot be reached by the simple addition of pluses and elimination of minuses from life." This describes Miss Lonelyhearts's efforts through the early chapters, his bouncing from one impulse to another in search of peace. That he does not find it is understandable, for as James remarks, "renunciation and despair . . . are our first step in the direction of the truth. There are two lives, the natural and the spiritual, and we must lose one before we can participate in the other." The early chapters of *Miss Lonelyhearts*, therefore, are a dialectic of loss. One by one Miss Lonelyhearts turns to possible *natural* outlets, the answers of this world, and one by one they prove inadequate. And in his frantic movement, Miss Lonelyhearts shows himself to be what James calls a "heterogeneous personality": "There are persons whose existence is little more than a series of zig-zags, as now one tendency and now another gets the upper hand." Bunyan (who is mentioned by West in his "Notes") is used by James as an example of a "Divided Self," a man religiously obsessed who could not, or would not, accept belief in Christ and was thrown into deepest despair by the struggle.

James considers the process of reunification a phenomenon not exclusively religious: "Religion is only one out of many ways of reaching unity." But whatever form it takes, it is "precisely the same psychological . . . event — a firmness, stability, and equilibrium succeeding a period of storm and stress and inconsistency." Furthermore, "In the spiritual realm there are . . . two ways, one gradual, the other sudden, in which inner unification may occur." Both Bunyan and Tolstoy are examples of "the gradual way," and West's specific reference to them makes sense, for Miss Lonelyhearts, too, is an instance of gradual unification, of wavering uncertainty before the final completion of self. The "calm" Miss Lonelyhearts experiences in the eighth chapter is a momentary respite from his sick morbidity, for in the following chapter he is still in bed: he "realized that his present sickness was unimportant. It was merely a trick by his body to relieve one more profound." And when he goes with Betty to the Connecticut farm, he experiences merely a relapse from the true process of unification going on inside him. The farm and the pastoral setting cannot make him well, because he is the more profound Sick Soul, and, as James notes, "no alteration of the environment" can cure this type. This explains Miss Lonelyhearts's reaction upon returning to the city: "When they reached the Bronx slums, Miss Lonelyhearts knew that Betty had failed to cure him and that he had been right when he had said that he could never forget the letters. He felt better, knowing this, because he had begun to think himself a faker and a fool."

Convinced now that environment is not the cause of his sickness, Miss

Lonelyhearts begins his quest for "humility." He finds that "the farther he got below self-laughter," the easier humility is to practice. This statement, coming at the beginning of the eleventh chapter, just before Miss Lonelyhearts meets Doyle in Delehanty's, is an indication of the progress he has made towards unification or "redemption." Back in the second chapter, Miss Lonelyhearts had said that self-laughter was a device he often used to protect himself: "'Ah, humanity. . . .' But he was heavy with shadow and the joke went into a dying fall. He tried to break its fall by laughing at himself." Self-laughter is a defense against taking oneself too seriously. Therefore, Miss Lonelyhearts's "humility"is not humility at all but a kind of egotistical obsession. The contradiction is apparent also in the statement that "Miss Lonelyhearts dodged Betty because she made him feel ridiculous." That he should want to keep from feeling ridiculous is the result of pride, not humility, for the truly humble man is filled already with a sense of his own ridiculousness.

More importantly, however, Miss Lonelyhearts in chapter thirteen has obviously been reborn:

> He thought of how calm he was. His calm was so perfect that he could not destroy it even by being conscious of it. In three days he had gone very far. It grew dark in the room. He got out of bed, washed his teeth, urinated, then turned out the light and went to sleep. He fell asleep without even a sigh and slept the sleep of the wise and the innocent. Without dreaming, he was aware of fireflies and the slop of oceans.

Miss Lonelyhearts's equilibrium is difficult to explain in the context of the novel alone. Just previously, he had failed miserably in haranguing the Doyles that "Christ is love," and afterwards, "He felt like an empty bottle, shiny and sterile." Miss Lonelyhearts then finds, suddenly, the lasting spiritual unification for which he has searched throughout the novel. What is its cause? Part of the answer, I think, lies in James's discussion of the subconscious maturing process which produces sometimes startling results. James comments on the general phenomenon, using the example of the recollection of a familiar name:

> Usually you help the recall by working for it, by mentally running over the places, persons, and things with which the word was connected. But sometimes this effort fails: you feel then as if the harder you tried the less hope there would be, as though the name were *jammed,* and pressure in its direction only kept it all the more from rising. And then the opposite expedient often succeeds. Give up the effort entirely; think of something altogether

different, and in half an hour the lost name comes sauntering into your mind, as Emerson says, as carelessly as if it had never been invited. Some hidden process was started in you by the effort, which went on after the effort ceased, and made the result come as if it came spontaneously.

Starbuck also describes this phenomenon: "The personal will must be given up. In many cases relief persistently refuses to come until the person ceases to resist, or to make an effort in the direction he desires to go." James gives Starbuck considerable credit for understanding this variety of conversion, known as "self-surrender," and his summary of Starbuck's exposition is excellent. Moreover, it very accurately describes what happens to Miss Lonelyhearts:

> Starbuck seems to put his finger on the root of the matter when he says that to exercise the personal will is still to live in the region where the imperfect self is the thing most emphasized. Where, on the contrary, the subconscious forces take the lead, it is more probably the better self *in posse* which directs the operation. Instead of being clumsily and vaguely aimed at from without, it is then itself the organizing centre. What then must the person do? "He must relax," says Dr. Starbuck — "that is, he must fall back on the larger Power that makes for righteousness, which has been welling up in his own being, and let it finish in its own way the work it has begun. . . . The act of yielding, in this point of view, is giving one's self over to the new life, making it the centre of a new personality, and living, from within, the truth of it which had before been viewed objectively."

Part of the reason for Miss Lonelyhearts's sudden "self-surrender" into conversion is that he has exhausted himself emotionally. His indifference is due to a draining of his energies. This is the reason he "had gone to bed again." It is also the reason he stands "quietly" in the center of the room when the drunken Shrike wants to fight. Miss Lonelyhearts is in the midst of what James calls the "state of temporary exhaustion [that] not infrequently forms part of the conversion crisis."

In the final chapters, Miss Lonelyhearts undergoes several of James's "varieties of experience," and, ironically, in the penultimate chapter, he is reborn into the realm of Healthy-Mindedness, where evil cannot reign triumphant. In "Miss Lonelyhearts and the party dress," he deliberately refuses to be affected by Betty's sharpness; instead he maintains a forced gaiety and tranquility. Now it is Miss Lonelyhearts who smiles, who overrides the harsh facts with the force of his will. He begs Betty to marry him, promises to take the job at the advertising agency, and in general attempts to coerce reality into pleasant shapes. When Betty tells him she is pregnant, he simply proposes marriage and takes her home. "He did not feel guilty. He did not feel. The rock was a solidification of his feeling, his conscience, his sense of reality, his self-knowledge." "Solidification" here does not mean realization, but rather a state opposite his earlier storm-and-stress when feeling, conscience, reality, and self-knowledge were all a mad, whirling jumble. As James describes the process,

> So long as the egoistic worry of the sick soul guards the door, the expansive confidence of the soul of faith gains no presence. But let the former faint away, even but for a moment, and the latter can profit by the opportunity, and, having once acquired possession, may retain it. Carlyle's Teufelsdröckh passes from the everlasting No to the everlasting Yes through a "Centre of Indifference."

The title of the last chapter, "Miss Lonelyhearts has a religious experience," alludes explicitly to James, and it is to this chapter and this experience that West points in his "Notes" when he describes Miss Lonelyhearts as "a priest of our time who has a religious experience." James devotes one of his later chapters to Mysticism, and what he has to say is directly related to the way West develops this final chapter. Essential to the mystic state, says James, is the penetration of the usual barriers separating the individual from the Absolute, whatever the Absolute may be for the given person: "In mystic states we both become one with the Absolute and we become aware of our oneness. This is the everlasting and triumphant mystical tradition, hardly altered by differences of clime or creed." This principle underlies Miss Lonelyhearts's experience in the final chapter:

> "Christ! Christ!" This shout echoed through the innermost cells of his body.
> He moved his head to a cooler spot on the pillow and the vein in his forehead became less swollen. He felt clean and fresh. His heart was a rose and in his skull another rose bloomed.
> The room was full of grace. A sweet, clean grace, not washed clean, but clean as the innersides of the inner petals of a newly forced rosebud.
> Delight was also in the room. It was like a gentle wind, and his nerves rippled under it like small blue flowers in a pasture.

He was conscious of two rhythms that were slowly becoming one. When they became one, his identification with God was complete. His heart was the one heart, the heart of God. And his brain was likewise God's.

God said, "Will you accept it, now?"

And he replied, "I accept, I accept."

The mystic experience, according to James, is always distinguished by two features: *Ineffability* ("it defies expression . . . no adequate report of its contents can be given in words") and *Noetic quality* ("insight into depths of truth unplumbed by the discursive intellect"); in addition, two other features are "usually found": *Transiency* ("half an hour, or at most an hour or two, seems to be the limit") and *Passivity* ("the mystic feels as if his own will were in abeyance . . . as if he were grasped and held by a superior power." These four characteristics apply accurately to Miss Lonelyhearts's mystic experience in the last chapter. The ineffability is seen in the imagistic description. The noetic quality is suggested (again through images) by "Christ is life and light" and "His heart was the one heart, the heart of God." Transiency is obvious: the entire description takes less than half a page. Likewise, Miss Lonelyhearts's will becomes the will of God, at least in Miss Lonelyhearts's mind: "He submitted drafts of his column to God and God approved them. God approved his every thought."

It is obvious, however, that Miss Lonelyhearts's mysticism in this final chapter is fatally mixed with Healthy-Mindedness, or at least one of the most striking features of Healthy-Mindedness, the belief in Mind-Cure. We have already noted how Miss Lonelyhearts seems to reverse roles with Betty in the penultimate chapter. There it is Betty who snaps, "What are you grinning at?" In the fourth chapter it was Miss Lonelyhearts who detested Betty's cheerfulness: "You have a smug smile; all you need is the pot belly." In the penultimate chapter, Miss Lonelyhearts has the "simplified mind"; and it is he who believes (foolishly) that everything will turn out all right if only he thinks it will, if only he believes strongly enough that he can override the unpleasant, ugly facts of the situation. He says he will take the advertising agency job: "He was not deliberately lying. He was only trying to say what she wanted to hear." And when Betty announces her pregnancy, Miss Lonelyhearts "begged the party dress to marry him, saying all the things it expected to hear, all the things that went with strawberry sodas and farms in Connecticut." This is a new Miss Lonelyhearts, completely different from the morbid person who earlier declared "he could never forget the letters."

James says that "Mind-Cure" is characterized by "an intuitive belief in the all-saving power of healthy-minded attitudes as such, in the conquering efficacy of courage, hope, and trust." The results of this attitude, according to James, are that

> the blind have been made to see, the halt to walk; lifelong in-
> valids have had their health restored. The moral fruits have been
> no less remarkable. The deliberate adoption of a healthy-minded
> attitude has proved possible to many who never supposed they
> had it in them; regeneration of character has gone on on an ex-
> tensive scale; and cheerfulness has been restored to countless homes.

Thus Miss Lonelyhearts can ignore the facts of the situation (for one thing, he does not love Betty) and believe that by wishing it, everything will be set right. It is this belief in mind-over-matter, Mind-Cure, which gets him killed.

Peter Doyle arrives to defend or restore his wife's "honor." When Miss Lonelyhearts sees him "working his way up the stairs," he is certain that "God had sent him so that Miss Lonelyhearts could perform a miracle and be certain of his conversion." "He would embrace the cripple and the cripple would be made whole again, even as he, a spiritual cripple, had been made whole." And so, "He rushed down the stairs to meet Doyle, with his arms spread for the miracle." The miracle, ironically, is death, not the "life and light" of Christ's crucifixion, and this is the final grotesque "religious experience" for Miss Lonelyhearts.

As for other varieties of religious experience, James distinguishes between "shallower" and "more profound" mystical states. Miss Lonelyhearts's orgiastic state in the final chapters is prefaced by some of the simpler mystic states. "The simplest rudiment of mystical experience," says James, is "that deepened sense of the significance of a maxim or formula which occasionally sweeps over one. . . . This sense of deeper significance is not confined to rational propositions. Single words, and conjunctions of words, effects of light on land and sea, odors and musical sounds, all bring it when the mind is tuned aright." West, in the third chapter of *Miss Lonelyhearts*, parallels James's "simplest rudiment of mystical experience." In this chapter Miss Lonelyhearts reads a passage from *The Brothers Karamazov* and immediately starts reflecting on Christ and "how dead the world is . . . a world of doorknobs." He recalls the religious impulses of his childhood: "when he shouted the name of Christ, something secret and enormously powerful" stirred in him.

Another type of "mystical" state, according to James, is the "consciousness produced by intoxicants and anesthetics, especially by alcohol. The sway of alcohol over mankind is unquestionably due to its power to stimulate the mystical faculties of human nature, usually crushed to earth by the cold facts and dry criticisms of the sober hour." In the fifth chapter Miss Lonelyhearts goes to Delehanty's speakeasy and "drank steadily." After a "train of stories . . . suggesting that what they all needed was a good rape," Miss Lonelyhearts "stopped listening" to his friends and drifts away in his mind to a recollection from his childhood:

> One winter evening, he had been waiting with his little sister for their father to come home from church. . . . he had gone to the piano and had begun a piece by Mozart. . . . His sister left her picture book to dance to his music. She had never danced before. She danced gravely and carefully, a simple dance yet formal. . . . As Miss Lonelyhearts stood at the bar, swaying lightly to the remembered music, he thought of children dancing. Square replacing oblong and being replaced by circle. Every child, everywhere; in the whole world there was not one child who was not gravely, sweetly dancing.

As a unifying vision, an image of perfection (oblong: square: circle), Miss Lonelyhearts's dream qualifies as one of James's lower forms of mystical experience. But, of course, this is an inadequate form of mysticism (as was the type mentioned before) and it ends with abrupt violence when Miss Lonelyhearts turns from the bar and gets punched in the mouth. The effect of the punch (besides a loosened tooth) is to bring him back to the world of reality: "His anger swung in large drunken circles. What in Christ's name was the Christ business? And children gravely dancing?" It is also in this chapter that a specific echo of James occurs in the remark by one of Miss Lonelyhearts's friends that "he's a leper licker. Shrike says he wants to lick lepers. Barkeep, a leper for the gent." This is almost certainly based on James's discussion of saintliness and the extremes to which holy people have gone in their love: "The nursing of the sick is a function to which the religious seem strongly drawn. . . . But in the annals of this sort of charity we find fantastic excesses of devotion recorded which are only explicable by the frenzy of self-immolation simultaneously aroused. Francis of Assisi kisses his lepers . . . St. John of God, and others are said to have cleansed the sores and ulcers of their patients with their respective tongues."

Finally, at the highest level, comes the direct mystical union with the Absolute, and earlier I quoted the passage in which Miss Lonelyhearts experiences it. Just before this union with God, Miss Lonelyhearts

fastened his eyes on the Christ that hung on the wall opposite
his bed. As he stared at it, it became a bright fly, spinning with
quick grace on a background of blood velvet sprinkled with tiny
nerve stars.

Everything else in the room was dead—chairs, table, pencils,
clothes, books. He thought of this black world of things as a fish.
And he was right, for it suddenly rose to the bright bait on
the wall. It rose with a splash of music and he saw its shining
silver belly.

West's description here is similar to James's discussion of *The Spiritual
Exercises* of Saint Ignatius Loyola. Ignatius, says James, tells "the disciple to
expel sensations by a graduated series of efforts to imagine holy scenes. The
acme of this kind of discipline would be a semi-hallucinatory mono-ideism—an
imaginary figure of Christ, for example, coming fully to occupy the mind.
Sensorial images of this sort, whether literal or symbolic, play an enormous
part in mysticism." West very carefully follows this pattern. First, Miss
Lonelyhearts expels extraneous, distracting sensations by fastening his eyes
on the crucifix. Immediately he sees a series of shifting images and symbols
which are clearly "semi-hallucinatory" and which culminate in the rising fish
image. This step is followed immediately by his realization that "Christ is
life and light."

The fish symbol, from ancient times a symbol for Christ, is most striking and corresponds remarkably to Starbuck's description of the sensation
of conversion. Most of Starbuck's subjects were not able to describe their
moment of conversion, but Starbuck notes that "two persons illustrated
graphically the process by drawing lines. In both, conversion was pictured
by rapidly ascending curves." The image of the fish rising in Miss Lonelyhearts's
consciousness so nearly conforms to Starbuck's "rapidly ascending curves"
that West may very well have been thinking of the earlier psychological work
at this point, despite West's claim that the imagery of *Miss Lonelyhearts* was
his own.

I earlier raised the problem of whether Miss Lonelyhearts is sick or saintly.
I think he is, indeed, "sick," but this opinion, too, needs to be qualified
by reference to James. In his opening lecture, "Religion and Neurology,"
James clearly states that he is not concerned with "individuals for whom
religion exists . . . as a dull habit," but instead he is interested in those "religious
geniuses" for whom religion is "an acute fever":

such religious geniuses have often shown symptoms of nervous
instability. Even more perhaps than other kinds of genius, religious

leaders have been subject to abnormal psychical visitations. Invariably they have been creatures of exalted emotional sensibility. Often they have led a discordant inner life, and had melancholy during a part of their career. They have known no measure, been liable to obsessions and fixed ideas; and frequently they have fallen into trances, heard voices, seen visions, and presented all sorts of peculiarities which are ordinarily classed as pathological. Often, moreover, these pathological features in their career have helped to give them their religious authority and influence.

West's development of Miss Lonelyhearts seems to parallel James's idea that exceptional religious experience is intrinsically combined with "peculiarities which are ordinarily classed as pathological." As much is implied in West's comment that while Miss Lonelyhearts is suffering from "maladjustment" he is also "a priest of our time who has a religious experience." Thus, at times we justifiably sympathize with Miss Lonelyhearts—in the scenes between him and Shrike, for instance. On the other hand, Miss Lonelyhearts is quixotic: despite his "great understanding heart," he can be detached, and sometimes even viciously contributes to the pain which so greatly distresses him. He hardly struggles at all when he commits adultery with Fay Doyle, so anxious is he for sexual release. And in one of the novel's perfectly ironic scenes he practically tears an old man's arm off thinking all the time that "he was twisting the arm of all the sick and miserable, broken and betrayed, inarticulate and impotent. He was twisting the arm of Desperate, Broken-hearted, Sick-of-it-all, Disillusioned-with-tubercular-husband." Miss Lonelyhearts here is reacting to his own sickness, frustration, and misery, his own sense of betrayal, his own inarticulateness and impotency, and West clearly intends us to see his violent actions as ironic contradictions.

Thus the question of Miss Lonelyhearts is not easily answered. But whether Miss Lonelyhearts is *ultimately* a religious man is a question that James would consider irrelevant. For James (and West as well I think) the final validity of religious belief and behavior is beyond understanding. James's pragmatic approach to the subject led him to disavow the possibility (and even the desirability) of understanding the supernatural origins and bases of religious experience. It was James's purpose to describe, from a scientific rather than a metaphysical point of view, that area of human experience known as "religious." Similarly, in *Miss Lonelyhearts*, West's concern with religious belief is limited to this world. Miss Lonelyhearts is driven to Christ because of the situation in this world and the need for answers here, not in the hereafter; he is not concerned with immortality, supernatural reality, or problems of theology. He is obsessed by the sterility of this "world of doorknobs," and his problem is partly whether belief in Christ is "too steep a price to pay" to bring this dead world to life. This is a pragmatic consideration, and it is precisely this point of view which James uses to determine the value of religious belief.

Briefly, James's argument is that "God is real since he produces real effects." By this James means that the belief in God causes men to have a variety of experiences (classified as "religious"), and experience is reality, at least the only reality open to understanding. Furthermore, religious experience is to be judged by its effects. Thus confession can be valid because "for him who confesses, shams are over and realities have begun; he has exteriorized his rottenness." Prayer, also, can justify itself apart from any supernatural order: "in certain environments prayer may contribute to recovery, and should be encouraged as a therapeutic measure." Sacrifice, on the other hand, when it consists of "burnt offerings and the blood of he-goats, is nothing but vain oblations."

When we apply this pragmatic Jamesian standard to *Miss Lonelyhearts*, we get a negative answer to the question of the value of religious experience. Miss Lonelyhearts's religious experience does not help him to cope with reality, even though he thinks it does. To the contrary, it leads him to his destruction, and by implication his death means additional suffering for Doyle, Betty, and the child within her. Light, therefore, is wrong when he argues that the message of *Miss Lonelyhearts* is that "the love and faith of Christ are the only solutions in which man can rest." In terms of the novel itself and from the standpoint of James's criteria, Miss Lonelyhearts's religious quest is a false one.

Words and Deeds

John R. May

The judgment of words and deeds is less explicit in *Miss Lonelyhearts* than it is in *As I Lay Dying;* it is nevertheless as central to the meaning of West's novel as it is to Faulkner's. Miss Lonelyhearts (Nathanael West gives his advice columnist no other name), whose obsessive concern is to discover some principle of order in the midst of the chaos of existence that he sees pointedly reflected in the letters written to him, is ultimately revealed deficient in both words and deeds. Shrike, the paper's feature editor who pushes the Miss Lonelyhearts column as a scheme to boost circulation, is a type of the loosed Satan who precedes the final catastrophe. The simple, almost stylized narrative that takes Miss Lonelyhearts through the stages of his quest for an answer to the problem of human suffering unfolds against a background of starkly opposed symbols of chaos and order.

The theme of spiritual quest is clear from the very beginning of the novel. Miss Lonelyhearts is a quarter of an hour away from his deadline, and he is still working on his leader; as usual he finds his words flat, insincere, and meaningless. Later, in trying to explain his problem to Betty, Miss Lonelyhearts constructs a parable perfectly descriptive of his own situation: "A man is hired to give advice to the readers of a newspaper. The job is a circulation stunt and the whole staff considers it a joke. . . . He too considers the job a joke, but after several months at it, the joke begins to escape him. He sees that the majority of the letters are profoundly humble pleas for moral and spiritual advice, that they are inarticulate expressions of genuine suffering." Miss Lonelyhearts realizes the impossibility of "finding the same joke funny thirty times a day for months on end," and so he rereads the letters he received that morning, "searching for some clue to a sincere

From *Toward a New Earth: Apocalypse in the American Novel.* © 1972 by the University of Notre Dame Press.

answer." Shrike has given him a piece of white cardboard with a blasphemous parody of the *anima christi* on it. It begins: "Soul of Miss L, glorify me." Miss Lonelyhearts has an intuition that Christ really *is* the answer; but since "Christ was Shrike's particular joke," he feels that he must "stay away from the Christ business" to keep from getting sick.

West articulates Miss Lonelyhearts's problem symbolically as a quest for order in the midst of chaos: "Miss Lonelyhearts found himself developing an almost insane sensitiveness to order. Everything had to form a pattern: the shoes under the bed, the ties in the holder, the pencils on the table . . . For a little while, he seemed to hold his own but one day he found himself with his back to the wall. On that day all the inanimate things over which he had tried to obtain control took the field against him. When he touched something, it spilled or rolled to the floor. . . . He fled to the street, but there chaos was multiple. Broken groups of people hurried past, forming neither stars nor squares." On the third day of his first illness, Miss Lonelyhearts has these thoughts: "Man has a tropism for order. Keys in one pocket, change in another. Mandolins are tuned G D A E. The physical world has a tropism for disorder, entropy. Man against nature . . . the battle of the centuries. Keys yearn to mix with change. Mandolins strive to get out of tune. Every order has within it the germ of destruction. All order is doomed, yet the battle is worth while."

Aside from several isolated and unambiguous images of apocalypse, there are key symbols of chaos and order in the novel that are fundamentally apocalyptic in meaning. The symbols of chaos are various aspects of nature, human artifacts, and especially human suffering—everything perhaps except human longing. There are also repeated dreams about and instances of violence that support the symbolism of chaos. The single symbol of order is the rock that Miss Lonelyhearts imagines himself becoming.

After his initial frustration in meeting his deadline, Miss Lonelyhearts goes to Delehanty's speakeasy. The gray sky, rubbed clean as if by an eraser, "held no angels, flaming crosses, olive-bearing doves, wheels within wheels." Later, after leaving Betty in a fit of self-righteous rage, "he felt as though his heart were a bomb, a complicated bomb that would result in a simple explosion, wrecking the world without rocking it." Again in Delehanty's he wears "the smile of an anarchist sitting in the movies with a bomb in his pocket."

Nature, supporting Miss Lonelyhearts's abhorrence of the idea and reality of entropy, never really does what it is supposed to. There are no signs of spring even though it is spring: "The decay that covered the surface of the mottled ground was not the kind in which life generates." Miss Lonelyhearts remembers that the previous year it had taken "all the brutality of July to torture a few green spikes through the exhausted dirt." Human artifacts conspire with nature to frighten and shock. The Mexican War obelisk in the park, although structurally a less than obvious suggestion that Miss Lonelyhearts should experiment with sex as a principle of order, seems on the verge of some crude stone orgasm as its shadow lengthens "in rapid jerks, not as shadows usually lengthen." The obelisk is "red and swollen in the dying sun, as though it were about to spout a load of granite seed." The skyscrapers "menaced the little park from all sides." Not even the countryside is different; it is clearly a reverse Eden. "The heavy, musty smell of old furniture and wood rot" makes Betty and Miss Lonelyhearts cough. The flies bother them, and an accidental noise frightens a deer back into the woods. The night noises are disturbing rather than pleasant for a change; and even with the blankets they are cold. Although spring is well advanced, the country is no different from the city: "In the deep shade there was nothing but death — rotten leaves, gray and white fungi, and over everything a funereal hush."

The analysis of the symbolism of chaos is incomplete without some understanding of Shrike's function in the novel as a warning sign of impending disaster. The *Random House Dictionary* describes a shrike as a predaceous bird that feeds on insects and smaller birds and kills more than it can eat. It has been pointed out that the name is close in sound to Christ, yet different enough to suggest the reverse even before one sees the full development of Shrike's role. He represents the demise of every human value; he is eager to recreate Miss Lonelyhearts in the image of his own appalling insensitivity and total cynicism. He has simply lost his humanity and thus is a perfect herald of final catastrophe in the tradition of the last loosing of Satan.

Certain descriptive touches contribute specifically to the interpretation of Shrike's portrait as demonic. Shrike, the cosmic joker, has chosen Christ as his "particular joke," as we have already mentioned. On his way to Delehanty's, Miss Lonelyhearts decides not to laugh at himself in his frustration because "Shrike was waiting at the speakeasy to do a much better job." One of Shrike's favorite tricks is "used much by moving-picture comedians — the dead pan." No matter how wildly he gesticulates or how excited his speech is, he tries never to change the expression on his face. He claims that it is suffering that drives him "into the arms of the Miss Farkises of this world." Miss Farkis is apparently one of many mistresses. He suffers because his wife was a virgin when she married him and "has been fighting ever since to remain one." Mary, on the other hand, says that the reason why Shrike allows her to go out with other men is "to save money." He allows other men to wine and dine her, then he reaps the sexual benefits of her mellow mood. It is not absolutely clear who is to be believed; one thing is clear, though, and that is that fidelity has little meaning in Shrike's world.

Shrike is the diabolical con man who tries each day to sell Miss Lonelyhearts on some new principle of order for his life, without of course even a hint of sincerity. Shrike recommends that Miss Lonelyhearts give his readers "something new and hopeful" rather than "the same old stuff," so he offers to dictate: "*Art is a Way Out . . . . Art is One of Life's Richest Offerings.* For those who have not the talent to create, there is appreciation." Later he advises Miss Lonelyhearts to "forget the crucifixion, remember the Renaissance." He is especially venomous in his parody of religion. When Miss Farkis announces that she is interested in the "new thomistic synthesis," Shrike asks her whether she has taken them for "stinking intellectuals" or "fake Europeans." He offers her instead, no doubt for Miss Lonelyhearts's benefit, a perfect synthesis for the machine age—a report on an adding machine used as a prayer wheel. Shrike begins a long diatribe called his "Passion in the Luncheonette, or the Agony of the Soda Fountain," which Miss Lonelyhearts understands rightly to be a seduction speech for the benefit of Miss Farkis. Shrike's visceral parable begins: "I am a great saint. . . . I can walk on my own water." He is also, of course, extremely drunk.

After his first sickness, Miss Lonelyhearts considers "how Shrike had accelerated his sickness by teaching him to handle his one escape, Christ, with a thick glove of words." Again at Delehanty's, after insisting that those who have faith are well, not sick, Shrike turns to Miss Lonelyhearts and says, "Come, tell us, brother, how it was that you first came to believe. Was it music in a church, or the death of a loved one, or, mayhap, some wise old priest?" Then, admitting how stupid it was of him not to realize that it was the letters, he proclaims that "the Miss Lonelyhearts are the priests of twentieth-century America." When Shrike reads Peter Doyle's letter containing Fay's accusation of attempted rape, Shrike tells the assembled friends, "This is only one more attempt against him by the devil. He has spent his life struggling with the arch fiend for our sakes, and he shall triumph. I mean Miss Lonelyhearts, not the devil." The gospel according to Shrike that follows, celebrating the long-suffering Miss Lonelyhearts, is nothing but unrelieved cynicism.

The diabolical tone of Shrike's portrayal becomes unmistakably clear when we consider the pattern of his seduction of Miss Lonelyhearts. It is the tripartite structure of the temptation of Jesus found in Matthew and Luke. Here, of course, is the special irony of West's small but vicious apocalypse. Miss Lonelyhearts is Jesus in the wilderness, weaving illusory order out of the chaos of Shrike's temptations, wanting desperately to resist but finally succumbing to Shrike's joke. Miss Lonelyhearts yields to the Pelagian temptation; he comes to believe that *he actually can do it*—bring order out of chaos himself.

Matthew and Luke are apparently both following the same tradition when they amplify Mark's less specific but more primitive account and thus describe Jesus' trial in the wilderness in terms of three (symbolically inclusive) temptations. Although the three temptations are the same in both Gospels, Luke's order (Lk. 4:1–13) inverts the second and third temptations of Matthew (Mt. 4:1–11). It is Luke's order that becomes the structural basis for Shrike's temptation. In Luke there is first of all the temptation to turn stones into bread, then the offer of all the kingdoms of the world if Jesus will do homage to Satan, and finally the temptation to presumption by casting himself from the pinnacle of the temple and expecting the support of God's angels.

Shrike's first temptation is a simply parody of Luke. He encourages Miss Lonelyhearts to give his readers stones rather than bread: "When they ask for bread don't give them crackers as does the Church, and don't, like the State, tell them to eat cake. Explain that man cannot live by bread alone and give them stones. Teach them to pray each morning: 'Give us this day our daily stone.'" The second temptation, Shrike's showing Miss Lonelyhearts the universal display of potential principles of order, is spread throughout the narrative. Yet as an ironic moment in Miss Lonelyhearts's ordeal in the wilderness, the panorama of possibilities is summarized in an episode that follows Miss Lonelyhearts's first illness. He has just articulated for himself the tension between chaos and order and the ascendancy of chaos. Shrike recommends the perennial answers to the destructive tendencies of nature. Viewed as potential principles of order, the answers are all escapes from reality. In presenting all the possibilities, Shrike is not above the cynical expression of preference; and thus he mentions in succession and rejects the soil, the South Seas, hedonism, art, suicide, and drugs. He finally reveals his trump card and equivalently asks Miss Lonelyhearts to adore his own special joke: "We are not men who swallow camels only to strain at stools. God alone is our escape. The church is our only hope, the First Church of Christ Dentist, where He is worshipped as Preventer of Decay. The Church whose symbol is the trinity new-style: Father, Son and Wirehaired Fox Terrier."

Shrike's temptations all coalesce in the third; the last temptation is the one that makes the acceptance of Shrike's offer possible because it is the temptation to believe that it really is possible to play God, of one's own accord to bring salvation to the multitudes, to save them through the order in one's own life. At the final party in his apartment, Shrike proposes that they play the game "Everyman his own Miss Lonelyhearts." Each person in the room is to answer one of the letters sent to Miss Lonelyhearts; and from the answer given, Miss Lonelyhearts will diagnose the person's moral ills. "Afterwards," Shrike promises, "he will lead you in the way of attainment." Although it may seem that the malicious Shrike is simply setting the stage to read Peter

Doyle's letter exposing Miss Lonelyhearts, the game announces the consummation of a process of temptation that has already taken place. Although he wanted to remain immune to the "Christ business," Miss Lonelyhearts is actually about to succumb to the ultimate degree of presumption when he reaches out to cure Peter Doyle as a confirmation of his identification of himself with God.

Miss Lonelyhearts's gradual fall into presumption is sketched in the developing symbolism of the rock. Throughout, Miss Lonelyhearts has been torn between the natural excitement that he experiences in shouting the name of Christ (and had since his youth in his father's church) and the perplexing fear that acceptance of the Christ answer would put him at Shrike's mercy. He gradually comes to realize that it is not Shrike who prevents him from embracing Christ, but his own lack of humility: "Men have always fought their misery with dreams. . . . He was capable of dreaming the Christ dream. He felt that he had failed at it, not so much because of Shrike's jokes or his own self-doubt, but because of his lack of humility." He vows, therefore, "to make a sincere attempt to be humble." and the outward sign of his essay at humility is his sanctimonious smile. He learns to smile at Shrike "as the saints are supposed to have smiled at those about to martyr them." Accepting Peter Doyle's invitation to dinner, he is "busy with his smile." When Fay Doyle makes a pass at him under the table, Miss Lonelyhearts "paid no attention to her and only broke his beatific smile to drink." Miss Lonelyhearts takes Peter's hand and continues "smiling and holding hands" until Fay calls them "a sweet pair of fairies."

The feigned humility and vapid smile effect Miss Lonelyhearts's increasing tendency to think of himself as a rock — solid, unperturbable, immune to the ravages of chaotic human existence, especially to Shrike. The feature editor bursts into Miss Lonelyhearts's apartment to invite him to his party; he is a single wave against a rock. "Shrike dashed against him, but fell back, as a wave that dashes against an ancient rock, smooth with experience, falls back. There was no second wave." Dunning Miss Lonelyhearts to join the party, Shrike becomes "a gull trying to lay an egg in the smooth flank of a rock, a screaming, clumsy gull." Mary Shrike sits on Miss Lonelyhearts's lap in the cab, "but despite her drunken wriggling the rock remained perfect." Miss Lonelyhearts withstands the ceaseless waves of Shrike's rhetoric: "What goes on in the sea is of no interest to the rock." The sea is a classic symbol of chaos, and here as throughout this passage the juxtaposition of the primitive symbols is patently apocalyptic.

Betty too could "see the rock he had become." His mind is touched curiously enough by the realization that Betty must dress up for special occasions; the rock, however, remains perfect. His *mind* is "the instrument with which he knew the rock." While they are planning for the future, Betty stops laughing and abruptly begins to cry: "He felt for the rock. It was still there; neither laughter nor tears could affect the rock. It was oblivious to wind or rain." The rock, tested and found perfect, is the "solidification of his feeling, his conscience, his sense of reality, his self-knowledge." When at the end his fever returns, the rock is no longer just a part of him; he *is* the rock. "The rock became a furnace."

Miss Lonelyhearts, like the reader, is perfectly prepared for the catastrophe that he creates. He has become the rock, and the rock is God—the foundation of all order, the eternally unchanged in the midst of the changing and changeable. He longs for a sign that will confirm his union with God. And so he decides to attempt a cure of Peter Doyle to prove to himself that "God approve[s] his every thought." The plan is to "embrace the cripple and the cripple would be made whole again, even as he, a spiritual cripple, had been made whole." Doyle comes to Miss Lonelyhearts's apartment, apparently with the intention of killing him for taking liberties with his wife. Miss Lonelyhearts rushes to enclose him in his saving embrace, but Doyle panics. The gun accidentally explodes, and Miss Lonelyhearts dies pathetically in the arms of the cripple he intended to cure.

He is judged for yielding to the ultimate temptation of making himself God; death is his ironic reward for succumbing, against his intentions, to Shrike's joke. Just as the words of his column were empty and meaningless, so were his deeds. He had presumed to do what no man can possibly do.

In *Miss Lonelyhearts*, the symbolism of catastrophe is developed regarding not only the warning signs of disaster, but also the end itself. The tone of impending disaster is established through the classical symbolism of threatening chaos. For Miss Lonelyhearts everything in life is chaotic save man's insatiable longing for order. The symbolism of chaos is composed of the concrete images of unseasonal nature, uncontrollable artifacts, and rampant human misery. Specifically, Shrike's role as tempter is a secular variation of the theme of the loosed Satan; this sign of impending disaster is a thinly disguised traditional symbol. Death is West's apocalyptic symbol of the end; it is the end not only for Miss Lonelyhearts but also, predictably, for all self-appointed saviors of men.

The rock is the primary symbol of order in the novel. Yet we would expect the symbol of order to be an indication of new life; in *Miss Lonelyhearts*, however, it is ironically the relevation of judgment. The rock is the sign of Miss Lonelyhearts's presumption; it is a traditional image for the unchanging fidelity of God. West's imagination projects no future for Miss Lonelyhearts;

he is the necessary victim of life's inevitable temptation to put an end to human misery. There is apparently no answer to the problem of evil—certainly not in presumption; there is only the frustration of irrepressible desire.

Freudian Criticism
and *Miss Lonelyhearts*

James W. Hickey

In this essay I will defend, through example, the legitimate place of Freudian theory as a tool of literary criticism and establish, through application of that theory, some new, constructive insights about the main character and central issues of Nathanael West's *Miss Lonelyhearts*.

It is hoped that the findings suggested by our Freudian approach to the novel will dispel Hyman's less disciplined use of Freudian theory and, less directly, show how Light's theory of genuine religious rebirth must be either reevaluated or totally rejected. Finally, the bulk of this essay is a response to the attacks of Randall Reid, with the intention of settling those issues which have been raised by the three major West critics (Hyman, Light and Reid himself) that defy solution without some acknowledgment of Freud's relevance.

Frederick J. Hoffman defines the correct application of Freudian criticism in appendix 1 to his book *Freudianism and the Literary Mind:*

> However inadequate this may be as a sketch of Freud's superbly exact descriptions, I introduce it here as a preliminary to examining its usefulness as a perspective upon literature. The two have in common what we may call a necessary language — language as the instrument of description becomes in the course of my discussion language as a system of strategies. Language is necessary at first to label and define; next, to put phenomena in order; then to characterize the nature of incentives for labelling and ordering; finally, in the most remarkable of its ranges of use, to effect changes in meaning, to represent situations as more complex than

From *Nathanael West: The Cheaters and the Cheated,* edited by David Madden. © 1973 by David Madden. Everett/Edwards, Inc., 1973.

they might be or are or ought to be. In the mind of a person endowed with every resource of language, the phenomena of psychic tension, conflict, drive, repression, are articulated and represented in a discourse at once psychologically just and remarkably subtle. I should like to suggest, therefore, that literature may be viewed and analyzed in terms of the verbal and metaphorical equivalents of the psyche and its behavior. Literature possesses a greater metaphoric freedom than psychology, or perhaps it has the license of its own audacity. But it is actively engaged in providing verbal and metaphorical equivalents of and elaborations upon the simply described behavior of the id, ego, and superego in their dynamic relationships. I can scarcely go on from here, to insist upon exact equivalents; it is perhaps as unwise to find oddities and egocentricities in literature as it is to accept literally biographical peculiarities as definitive explanations of achieved works of art. To locate an author's id, ego, superego, etc., in either characters or lines is to violate the subtlety of their necessary arrangements. My purpose is, instead, to explain the complexities of literary work as the results of symbolic actions which report and reflect on a high level of linguistic articulateness and subtlety the basic tensions, balances, imbalances, repressions, and compensations of psychic energies within a system such as Freud has described.

As a guideline for the productive application of Freudian criticism, the statement closely parallels my interpretation of West's own observations on the proper (and improper) uses of Freudian theory. It is generally within these limits that this study of *Miss Lonelyhearts* will be carried out.

If we are to maintain the position that the text of *Miss Lonelyhearts* be treated as a written record of ML's consciousness, it follows easily and of necessity that we regard the themes of the book with more than mere literary appreciation, as symptoms of ML's disturbance. As such, they stress those objects and opinions with which ML is psychically involved—just as these motivations, abstracted as themes, define the issues of the novel. For our purposes, this approach does not demand that we exclude non-psychological interpretation on a more obviously literary level; rather, it is merely a means of more easily revealing the contextual relevance of Freudian theory.

Since we have already raised the question of ML's subjective interpretation of reality, the natural starting place for our study is a definition of his reality. Contextually, West reveals this in the first chapter as ML reads the letters from his lovelorn "congregation." The reality with which ML's ego must deal is filled with chaotic disorder and suffering. Like ML, we are shocked and distressed by the inarticulate pleas of Sick-of-it-all, Desperate, and Harold S. But, in our first reading of the novel, we fail to understand the function of these letters for ML. Surely ML has received letters from girls with pimples or dating problems. Yet he prefers to dwell on the letters from a girl with no nose and a boy whose idiot sister has been raped. There is obviously something about the hopelessness of these situations which ML finds attractive, no matter how much he may deny it consciously. West resolves this incongruity for us immediately: "He stopped reading. Christ was the answer, but, if he did not want to get sick, he had to stay away from the Christ business. Besides, Christ was Shrike's particular joke." With concentrated precision, West thus introduces ML's pathological relationship to "the Christ business." ML has selected these letters because they permit him to indulge in his Christ fantasies. They are prayers for salvation which have been sent to him, the tabloid priest, but which he uses only to confirm his own inability to achieve the Christ identity of his dreams. Past attempts to achieve such a self-image have evidently resulted in emotional and physical illness which ML cannot ignore but refuses to recognize as pathological. It is this tension between ML's craving for the Christ identity and his psychological rejection of it which is at the core of the book's action. The "resolution" of this dilemma in the last chapters finds ML terrifyingly achieving his fantasy.

The above quotation further establishes Shrike's attitude as a sort of alter ego to ML. The novel has already opened with Shrike's shocking parody of the *anima christi,* but, more subtly, the parody makes us aware of the role which ML has assumed. Not only does it substantiate ML's perverse relationship to Christ, but it reveals that others are aware of his mania as well. Through his constant jibes, Shrike will not permit ML to escape into the fantasy worlds of art, nature, hedonism, or suicide. Although he is treated unsympathetically, Shrike's unrelenting vision of reality is certainly less fanciful than ML's. Shrike, too, is confronted with the misery of humanity, but it is an easy misconception to assume that Shrike's surface callousness negates his despair. Indeed, it confirms Shrike's self-tortured involvement as, like the wounded animal of a later chapter, he tears at the wound to hurt the pain. In this respect, Shrike is interpreted in ML's consciousness as a coalition of ML's alter ego, that which reminds ML that he has not and will not realize his Christ dream. If Shrike is depicted as a jeering, sniveling sadist, it is because that is the way in which ML's demented consciousness perceives him.

The ultimate pathos, and perhaps, nobility of Shrike lies in his own awareness that he too lacks any vision of salvation. He is only too aware of his own futility. When conversing with Goldsmith, a lesser mirror of himself, Shrike observes: " 'Goldsmith, you are a nasty product of this unbelieving age. You cannot believe, you can only laugh. You take everything with a bag of salt and forget that salt is the enemy of fire as well as of ice. Be warned, the salt you use is not Attic salt, it is coarse butcher's salt. It doesn't preserve; it kills.' " Shrike is a man condemned to having few or no illusions about himself and the world around him; ML is condemned to having his vision obscured by just such illusions. Podhoretz suggests that "West regards Shrike's cynicism as a stunted form of wisdom." In many respects, Shrike thus assumes the additional role of chorus. Shrike and the newspapermen at Delehanty's speakeasy, for all their obscene cynicism, are truly reporters of the "real" reality which ML cannot face, and we should pay attention to them, even if ML will not. It is a sordid reality which is as much defined by ML's distorted fantasies as it is by Shrike's outrageous perspective. West underscores this disquieting reality by thematically insisting that we recognize the degree to which fantasy—as corrupting as it is necessary for survival— constitutes our own vision of reality.

ML has tried to distract himself from this terrifying vision by con- structing the two sub-realities: the Christ business and order.

The brief chapter "Miss Lonelyhearts and the Lamb" illustrates most completely the extent of his Christ fixation by describing ML's room and permitting the main character to lapse into a hysterical dream which recalls a college experience. The chapter seems to have been written specifically for the Freudian critic.

Within the barren confines of his dark, womb-like room, ML has spiked an ivory Christ to the wall to make its suffering more "real," but the desired effect has failed because he has not nailed Christ (nor himself) to the wall— merely a hard, unfeeling piece of ivory. The obvious conclusions to be made here concern not only ML's desire constantly to fuse his own suffering with the divine passion of Christ. The ultimate failure of the gesture to achieve the desired sensational projection confirms his own failure to experience this fantasy, much less the actual suffering of his readers. ML will finally accomplish his identification with Christ once he accepts the self-image of the imperturb- able rock, which is as incapable of suffering and emotion as the ivory statute.

As the chapter continues, we discover that ML blames Shrike for his inability to achieve the Christ dream, thus substantiating the subjective vision of the narrative.

> He realized, even if Shrike had not made a sane view of this Christ
> business impossible, there would be little use in his fooling himself.
> His vocation was of a different sort. As a boy in his father's church,
> he had discovered that something stirred in him when he shouted
> the name of Christ, something secret and enormously power-

ful. He had played with this thing, but had never allowed it
to come alive.

He knew now what this thing was — hysteria, a snake whose
scales are tiny mirrors in which the dead world takes on a semblance
of life. And how dead the world is . . . a world of doorknobs.
He wondered if hysteria were really too steep a price to pay for
bringing it to life.

If nothing else, the passage reveals that ML is not entirely unaware of his
mental condition. Passing the blame to Shrike, he can admit that his relationship to the Christ business is not "sane." He further reveals that he has
been suffering from attacks of hysteria since childhood, but he only feebly
rationalizes the condition as something which sets his vocation apart. His
hysteria takes the shape of a phallus whose mirror-like scales reflect the dead
world which ML apparently perceives. The movement of the phallus-snake
permits the world to take on the "semblance of life" while the phallus itself
is obscured by the reflection of doorknobs. The doorknobs, which in a subsequent fit he will bring to life as a magician leading prayers, tie in directly
with the breast fixation which he and (his interpretation of) the other characters
share. The memory, with all its Freudian finery, combines the hysterical vision
of the young ML with his father's church. As the child rants Christ's name
deliriously, he is establishing for the Freudian reader his view of his relationship with his father.

Tragically, ML has experienced this hysteria so often that he has helplessly
made the fit a ritual in itself, telling himself that he is governing it ("He
had played with this thing, but he had never allowed it to come alive") whereas
in truth it has all but sapped his sanity. ML performs the rite by staring
at the obscene crucifix and chanting Christ's name until he is unconscious.
West's third-person observation, "For him, Christ was the most natural of
excitements," is certainly not a cruel Shrikean joke. It is ML's own rationaliza-
tion of the act over which he has no control. More importantly, it is the
key to ML's impotent relationships with Betty and Mary Shrike. Sex with
them and the gross Fay Doyle is unnatural, theatrical to him. His most complete passion is that of and with Christ, an act of narcissistic homosexuality.
But even in this fit, he cannot find fruition of his fantasy, for his "performance" of a prayer as a magician recalls Shrike's *anima christi*. Again, while
ML would blame Shrike for this disruption of ML's dream, it is more clearly
ML's own egotism which acknowledges the prayer as being directed to its
proper god. Once more, Shrike's apparent irreverence turns out to be a revealed
truth. Similarly, in this second prayer, Christ's blood is not transubstantiated
from wine but from boric acid. Such is the destructive essence of ML's Christ.

West uses this prayer and an earlier reference to *The Brothers Karamazov* to establish the religious concept of Christ as the lamb of God. He then shifts the dream to a Freudian nightmare of castration anxiety and self-destruction. The failure to complete the decapitation (castration) of the sacrificial lamb (ML/Christ), the broken sword, the hysterical fleeing, the final crushing of the head with the stone, the swarming flies and altar of flowers — all may be interpreted as both religious and Freudian symbols. A momentary glance at Jung's concept of the rebirth archetype reveals yet another means of fusing the spiritual with the psychological. West manipulates the fantasy like a giant pun as Jud(as) Hume purchases the lamb that is to be slaughtered, as they chant obscene verses of "Mary Had a Little Lamb," as the violent (frenzied) sacrifice takes place on a hill, as the remains of the lamb become Lord of the flies (Beelzebub), and so on. Here, and at the close of the novel, the Jungian rebirth ritual is frustrated in that there is only destruction of a feeble divinity in an atmosphere of omnipresent sterility.

ML's obsession with order is explored in the following chapter. The opening paragraphs of this section offer a different, but equally frightening, form of ML's mental imbalance.

> Miss Lonelyhearts found himself developing an almost insane sensitiveness to order. Everything had to form a pattern: the shoes under the bed, the ties in the holder, the pencils on the table. When he looked out of a window, he composed the skyline by balancing one building against another. If a bird flew across this arrangement, he closed his eyes angrily until it was gone.
>
> For a little while, he seemed to hold his own but one day he found himself with his back to the wall. On that day all the inanimate things over which he had tried to gain control took the field against him. When he touched something, it spilled or rolled to the floor. The collar buttons disappeared under the bed, the point of the pencil broke, the handle of the razor fell off, the window shade refused to stay down. He fought back, but with too much violence, and was decisively defeated by the spring of the alarm clock.
>
> He fled to the street, but there chaos was multiple. Broken groups of people hurried past, forming neither stars nor squares. The lamp-posts were badly spaced and the flagging was of different sizes. Nor could he do anything with the harsh clanging sound of street cars and the raw shouts of hucksters. No repeated group of words would fit their rhythm and no scale could give them meaning.

He stood quietly against a wall, trying not to see or hear. Then he remembered Betty. She had often made him feel that when she straightened his tie, she straightened much more. And he had once thought that if the world were larger, were *the* world, she might order it as finally as the objects on her dressing table.

Once again, West's understatements in the first sentence of the chapter reflects not so much a lack of awareness on the author's behalf as it does ML's attempt to rationalize his irrational behavior.

One of the reasons that this mania for order is so perplexing rises from the fact that it is not so easy to discover its cause. Whereas the Christ complex is apparently a manifestation of ML's phrenetically ambiguous relationship to his father, there seems to be no set Freudian formula to explain away this second symptom. Rather than reveal its motivation here, it may be more important to concentrate on its significance at this stage of the novel.

The first point to emphasize concerns ML's reaction to his own irrational behavior. This behavior pattern unobtrusively becomes a theme of the novel itself, despite ML's projection of it as the fault of others. Even when ML is reading the pathetic letters in the first chapter—at which time we share his alleged horror and are most willing to identify with him as protagonist—the action of the sequence is held together by ML's inability to enjoy a cigarette. "The cigarette was imperfect and refused to draw. Miss Lonelyhearts took it out of his mouth and stared at it furiously. He fought himself quiet, then lit another one." The incident passes, presumably induced by ML's distress over the letters. However, in light of the passage on the pages quoted above, ML's furious reaction indicates his total loss of self-control. His irrationality complements perfectly the faulty cigarette which obviously connotes impotence. Similarly, ML maintains that he wishes to be free from the sordid confessions of the masses; yet, when the clean old man refuses to bare his soul, ML attacks him viciously and violently until hit with a chair from behind. The same behavior pattern is evident, to greater or lesser extents, in his recollections of the lamb sacrifice and his fondling of Betty's breasts. If nothing else, it is a physical extension of ML's aberration.

The other important point to be learned from the lengthy description of ML's mania for order concerns his second response. He turns to Betty, his fiancée, whom he regards as the personification, the very embodiment of order. Considering ML's complex sexual attitude, it is important to be fully aware of Betty's role as love-object through ML's compulsion for order.

The chapter continues to reveal that Betty offers little more for ML as a love-object than an outlet for his violent frustration. Looking to her for an escape from his own irrationality, his guilt, frustration and anxiety prevent him from expressing any true emotions to her. Though he and the reader do not at this point of the novel know why, ML can only relate to Betty with theatricality and sadism. It is only in a more sordid setting that ML liminally indicates the subtle relationship between Betty and ML's mania for order. Rather than discuss Betty's intricate role in ML's demented perception, however, we would do well to probe more deeply into ML's other hysterical confrontations with, literally, mental disorder.

The chapter "Miss Lonelyhearts in the Dismal Swamp" is ambiguous in structure. It begins by stating that, immediately following his seduction of Fay Doyle, ML falls victim to a two-day-long session of vomiting and coma, culminating in an elaborate fantasy. ML imagines himself in front of a pawnshop window and begins mentally to order the secondhand items he sees there into geometric shapes, beginning with a phallus and culminating with a cross. The pawnshop articles, like his letters, fascinate him because they are "the paraphenalia of suffering" so vital to his psychotic vision. As with the Christ dream, his struggle with order seems a hopeless expression of his own impotent futility. Man's tropism for order is directly opposed in ML's mind to Nature's "tropism for disorder, entropy." "Every order has within it the germ of destruction," ML muses. "All order is doomed, yet the battle is worth while." Again, as with the Christ delusion, there is the association of the symptom's expression with destruction.

ML's fantasies dissolve into a revolting hallucination of a polluted ocean. The image, which Freudians would interpret as a feminine symbol, offers the perfect cue for Betty's timid return to the action of the novel. With chicken soup in hand, his girlfriend offers advice to him, a lovelorn columnist, and tries to soothe him with stories of her idyllic childhood. With a flash, Shrike suddenly replaces her in a dream ["Betty left without saying good-by"]. Shrike taunts ML with the various forms of futile escapism open to him and predictably concludes with the Christ dreams. The whole chapter assumes a sense of nonreality as the images of Betty and Shrike interchange and they recite their philosophies to the hysterical ML. Indeed, it is entirely possible that the chapter is itself complete fantasy, as the reality of ML's delusions take an increasing hold on ML's conscious faculties. Even if the visitors have actually been present—for Betty appears to him every day following this incident—it is important to stress once more that, as interpreted by ML's consciousness through the narrative of West's words, the Betty and Shrike described to us have little relationship to the actual characters as they exist outside ML's consciousness.

Freudian theory offers a helpful insight into the more general explanation of ML's coma and hysteria. While a general theory cannot pinpoint the precise motivation for ML's mania for order, it can indicate the pathological future of the patient.

> In estimating the influence of organic disease upon the distribution of the libido . . . it is universally known, and seems to us a matter of course, that a person suffering organic pain and discomfort relinquishes his interest in the things of the outside world, in so far as they do not concern his suffering. Closer observation teaches us that at the same time he withdraws libidinal interest from his love-objects: so long as he suffers, he ceases to love. . . . The sick man withdraws his libidinal cathexes back upon his ego, and sends them forth again when he recovers.

In the long run, of course, ML is never to recover, but the quotation does shed light on the chapter following this nightmare in which ML and Betty go to the country and make love without any inhibitions one morning. That ML voluntarily makes love to Betty presents a stiff challenge to the theory of ML's alleged homosexuality and, more directly, offers still greater evidence that Betty holds an underestimated role in ML's psychosexual perception of his unique, distorted reality.

The final chapters of the novel disclose how ML's hysteria and organic suffering become fused into total insanity. Describing ML's activity after he has returned to the city and met Peter Doyle, the chapters depend intricately upon Freud's quotation above to illustrate the process of disintegration in ML's mind. It is here that Peter Doyle, the ineffectual cripple, becomes ML's second genuine love-object. Just as ML seeks comfort from Betty as a symbol of natural order, he seeks from Peter Doyle the fruition of his Christ fantasy and his own ambiguous sex identity.

We do not need Shrike's bitter sarcasm to tell us that Peter Doyle is a living symbol of the sordid suffering humanity who seek salvation in ML's lovelorn column. As such, he offers ML the opportunity to play out his Christ fantasy with the silent understanding that he, Doyle, be permitted to indulge in his own role as this crippled symbol. A piecemeal collage of society's depravity ("He looked like one of those composite photographs used by a screen magazine in guessing contests"), Doyle's physical unfitness is said to excite ML even as the two men stare silently at each other. West makes it clear that ML is attracted to Doyle physically and stirred not by his pathetic sob story on which he cannot even concentrate, but by the relationship they are mutually sharing.

> When the cripple finally labored into speech, Miss Lonelyhearts
> was unable to understand him. He listened hard for a few minutes
> and realized that Doyle was making no attempt to be understood.
> He was giving birth to groups of words that lived inside him
> as things. . . .
>   Like a priest, Miss Lonelyhearts turned his face slightly away. . . .
>   Doyle's damp hand accidentally touched his under the table.
> He jerked away, but then drove his hand back and forced it to
> clasp the cripple's. . . . He did not let go, but pressed it firmly
> with all the love he could manage. At first the cripple covered
> his embarrassment by disguising the meaning of the clasp with
> a handshake, but he soon gave in to it and they sat silently, hand
> in hand.

The scene has obvious sexual overtones and establishes for ML a means by which he may express his libidinal frustration through his Christ complex.

Again, the scene in the country with Betty raises some difficult problems. How does she fit into this new homosexual relationship? Why does ML reject aggressively—in an almost manly fashion—the new advances of Fay Doyle? With the development of his relationship with Peter Doyle, how can ML rationalize his plans to marry Betty? And where does the reinforced Christ business fit into ML's new psychological position?

Clearly, some of the answers lie in ML's final attack of hysteria. When presumably counseling Peter and Fay Doyle, ML tries his God-is-the-answer pitch "by becoming hysterical." Although it fails to work when he would wish it to, the hysteria does manifest itself once ML has escaped from Fay's attempt to seduce and rape him. As before, he falls into a three-day coma (the Christian reference is obvious) and is completely lost in the "reality-world" of his own hysterical fantasy. "Without dreaming," ML experiences a surreal hallucination and, when interrupted by Shrike and his friends, maintains the psychotic identity of his ivory Christ. A reaction to the fact of his latent homosexuality having come to the surface of his consciousness, ML defensively establishes his identity as an impervious rock which is incapable of emotion of any kind. The battle has been lost and ML's slightest glimmers of sanity have been obliterated by his all-encompassing schizophrenic hysteria. Naturally, the demented consciousness of ML, as revealed by West's words, is not aware of the perverse manifestations of this new identity. Thus it is that, in keeping with the other descriptions of ML's psychotic perception, West never openly states, as ML's consciousness, that there is anything strange or neurotic about ML's condition. In fact, despite West's indirect indications to the contrary, James F. Light accepts, with the demented ML, his long-awaited religious reincarnation. It becomes increasingly obvious that nothing could be farther from the facts of the case.

We are treating West's novel as an extension of ML's consciousness; as ML's thoughts register those details which most fascinate him, it must be observed that the people with whom ML surrounds himself confront him constantly with breasts and breast imagery. Shrike estimates Miss Farkis's intelligence by the size of her busts; Mary Shrike recites the plight of her Mother's breast cancer as her own breasts are being fondled by ML in the doorway of her apartment; Fay Doyle's balloon breasts are a notable contrast to Betty's "pink-tipped thumbs"; and, when trying to arouse himself enough to phone Mary Shrike for a date, ML concentrates on a pair of painted breasts in a mineral water advertisement — but even this does not work. As previously suggested, the breast imagery becomes expressed more subtly in the sub-conscious fantasies which ML experiences while undergoing an attack of hysteria. Recalling ML's helpless, almost unconscious submission to a violent expression of his frustration when confronted with the imperfect cigarette and, later, the clean old man, it is interesting to note that ML's dream breasts, doorknobs, symbolize a dead world, and that ML can consider them living, can bring them to life only by making them bleed and thus become something other than doorknobs.

This association of breasts with violence is more directly expressed in his relationship with Betty. Terrified by his hysteria, ML rushes to Betty for comfort and order, but "by the time he got there, his panic had turned to irritation." Unable to talk (his tongue here shares the image West later uses to describe Betty's breasts — that of the fat thumb), ML defensively seeks some means of rationalizing his inability to behave normally with Betty. Unable to project the blame onto Betty, he tries to evoke her contempt so that he *will* be able to. It becomes clear that this is the role ML would have Betty play for him. He has avoided her since she began describing their dream-perfect marriage, suggesting strongly to us that ML has little interest in such a relationship. Nervous and still irritated, ML fondles Betty's breasts for want of anything else to do.

> She made no sign to show that she was aware of his hand. He would have welcomed a slap, but even when he caught at her nipple, she remained silent.
>
> "Let me pluck this rose," he said, giving a sharp tug. "I want to wear it in my buttonhole."
>
> Betty reached for his brow. "What's the matter?" she asked. "Are you sick?"
>
> He began to shout at her, accompanying his shouts with gestures

that were too appropriate, like those of an old-fashioned actor.

"What a kind bitch you are. As soon as one acts viciously, you say he's sick. . . . Well, I'm not sick. I don't need your damned aspirin. I've got a Christ complex. Humanity . . . I'm a humanity lover."

. . . Instead of answering, she raised her arm as though to ward off a blow. She was like a kitten whose soft helplessness makes one ache to hurt it.

The passage suggests that ML's decision to play with Betty's breasts is not so much out of boredom, itself not particularly a natural motivation, but to force her to respond violently towards him. Although she reacts with frustrating kindness, that she has reacted at all permits ML to act out his anxiety. His speech reveals that he is consciously aware of his perverse behavior but that he must blame her for his actions. He further consciously rejects the notion that his malady is physically oriented or that it may be helped by wonder drugs. He even acknowledges his Christ complex in this fit of rage, but he must quickly associate this condition with a lesser symptom, one which he can handle objectively and which permits a favorable self-image. He has, therefore, disclosed his use of humanity as an overwhelming symbol of suffering which he can manipulate until he becomes its victim. By projecting his Christ complex into this grab-bag of impersonal grievances, ML has created the illusion of objectivity; more correctly, he has escaped the subjective implications of his own neuroses. By identifying himself as a humanity lover instead of a demented "Christ nut," ML affords himself a self-image with which he can play more gratifyingly and on which he may depend when threatened with anxiety and/or hysteria. However, West interjects that such an image is merely a performance, which fact ML liminally knows but cannot rationally accept. The fantasy which ML is trying to convince both Betty and himself of is further destroyed by ML's actions as he relates it. While professing to be a lover of humanity, he is menacingly on the brink of violence and "aches" with the compulsion to attack Betty as he has done to the lamb in college, a small frog in his memory, and the clean old man in Delehanty's.

The incident serves many purposes in the novel. It dramatically unifies the themes of Christ complex, order obsession, and hysteria through the sadistic, semi-literal rape of Betty. Furthermore, it defines ML's perverse dependency on Betty as consoler and scapegoat. ML physically acts out his mental disorder and subsequently explains it until he arrives so close to the truth of the matter that he must retreat to a self-image that is becoming less and less acceptable. Sexual ambivalence is also physically and emotionally in evidence. While performing an act of passion, ML is motivated by hatred rather than the common concept of love; while tearing at Betty and verbally rejecting her, ML is confirming his emotional dependence on her.

"I love you."

"And I love you," he said. "You and your damned smiling through tears."

The role ML has made for Betty demands an innocence which cannot help but further frustrate ML, thus creating a literal vicious cycle. At this point of the novel, ML's fondling of Betty's breasts permits him to indulge the neuroses that must be expressed while it protects him from any genuine heterosexual experience which could threaten his sexual identity.

Breasts again assume this symbol of frustration and desired non-intimacy when ML takes Mary Shrike to El Gaucho, the nightclub of sordid romanticism. By her husband's admission, Mary Shrike is frigid, yet she uses her breasts to excite ML. In this way, she personifies ML's vision of the dead world of doorknobs. It is revealing that she is not only frigid but that she is the only woman other than Betty who has tolerated ML prior to Fay Doyle. The marriage of these two qualities make Mary a strangely suitable "love"-object for the sexually ambivalent ML.

ML's petting sessions with Mary Shrike are strikingly similar to the one with Betty and ML's interpretation of them substantiates our conclusions about his role with heterosexuality.

> When he kissed Shrike's wife, he felt less like a joke. She returned his kisses because she hated Shrike. But even there Shrike had beaten him. No matter how hard he begged her to give Shrike horns, she refused to sleep with him.
>
> Although Mary always grunted and upset her eyes, she would not associate what she felt with the sexual act. When he forced this association, she became angry. He had been convinced that her grunts were genuine by the change that took place in her when he kissed her heavily. Then her body gave off an odor that enriched the synthetic flower scent she used behind her ears and in the hollows of her neck. No similar change ever took place in his own body, however. Like a dead man, only friction could make him warm or violence make him mobile. . . .
>
> He tried to excite himself into eagerness by thinking of the play Mary made with her breasts. She used them as the coquettes of long ago had used their fans. One of her tricks was to wear a medal low down on her chest. Whenever he asked to see it instead of drawing it out she leaned over for him to look. Although

he had often asked to see the medal, he had not yet found out
what it represented.

But the excitement refused to come. If anything, he felt colder
than before he had started to think of women. It was not his line.
Nevertheless, he persisted in it, out of desperation. . . .

The first paragraph shows the complex of motivations surrounding their relationship. For both of them, the affair seems to be dominated by a direct de-
fiance against Shrike. As with ML, Mary's performance does not appear to
be associated with lovemaking. She seems to ignore ML's advances and to
find her own gratification in the grotesque gestures of their embrace. Her
sexual identity is one of negation: she achieves her perverse fulfillment through
her denial to Shrike and ML and gratifies her ego with the self-image of a tease.

ML uses her aberration to his advantage. His propositions are delivered
as lifelessly as are his gestures of affection.

"The way to be gay is to make other people gay," Miss
Lonelyhearts said. "Sleep with me and I'll be one gay dog."

The defeat in his voice made it easy for her to ignore his re-
quest and her mind sagged with his. . . . .

"Sleep with me," he said.

"No, let's dance."

"I don't want to. Tell me about your mother."

"She died leaning over a table. The pain was so terrible that
she climbed out of bed to die."

Mary leaned over to show how her mother had died. . . .

He clearly does not expect her to sleep with him, nor is he unwilling to
permit her to become yet another confessor to him. Mary acts out her mother's
death as she relates it, thus using ML to fulfill her own breast fixation whose
roots are obviously an outgrowth of her mother's breast cancer. Thus, the
two of them share an intimacy of perversions. As Mary chatters on, ML
concentrates on the medal. "He saw that there was a runner on it, but was
unable to read the inscription." The medal may be interpreted as a symbol
of ML's attitude toward heterosexuality. As with his propositions to sleep
with Mary, ML asks to see the medal but has no real knowledge of it, repeating
the pattern of aggression and non-experience. It is appropriate that the medal,
so overtly a part of their sexual relationship, should depict a runner. Mary
Shrike's breasts, an ambivalent combination of enticement and malignancy,
symbolize the threat of heterosexuality for ML, much as the deadness of her
body complements his own.

West jokes cruelly when he puns on the word "gay" in ML's proposition to Mary Shrike, but it is with some of the most remarkable imagery in the novel that West outlines ML's perverse sexuality. Sitting in the park trying to decide whether or not he should phone Mary Shrike for a date, ML stares at a phallic obelisk which his mind brings to life through an erotic hallucination. "The stone shaft cast a long, rigid shadow on the walk in front of him. He sat staring at it without knowing why until he noticed that it was lengthening in rapid jerks, not as shadows usually lengthen. He grew frightened and looked up quickly at the monument. It seemed red and swollen in the dying sun, as though it were about to spout a load of granite seeds." West's imagery reveals the way in which ML's mental condition is controlling his perception of "real" reality, extending poetically and actuality. The image not only serves as a projection of ML's psychosexual frustration but it is also a preparation for his pathological fulfillment of identity through the self-image of a rock. Elsewhere, West extends ML's sexual attitude through images in the "real" world when, while phoning Fay Doyle, ML stares at a pair of disembodied genitals which have been carved on the wall. In both cases, the imagery is masterfully connotative of ML's sexual deadness, the latter more directly alluding to ML's castration anxiety.

As has been suggested, ML's castration anxiety is most apparent in the chapter "Miss Lonelyhearts and the Lamb." The lamb sacrifice parallels, directly and by implication, that of a child performing an ancient totem ritual, as interpreted by Freud: "It is true that in the case of little Arpad . . . his totemic interests did not arise in direct relation with his Oedipus complex but on the basis of its narcissistic precondition, the fear of castration. . . . The same part is played by the father alike in the Oedipus and castration complexes— the part of a dreaded enemy to the sexual interests of childhood. . . . His attitude towards his totem animal was superlatively ambivalent: he showed both hatred and love to an extravagant degree." Freud's observations here are important to any literary critic, if only to disprove Hyman's dependency on the Oedipus complex as the motivation of ML's delirium. While accounting for ML's castration anxiety and his ambivalence toward his love-objects, the passage further helps to define ML's relationship to his father. Thus Freud presents us with the key by which we may better comprehend the meaning of ML's hysterical recollection while sifting out the symptoms which are at the core of his neurosis. It becomes increasingly apparent that ML's latent homosexuality, overt narcissism, delusions of grandeur, and desire to emulate his father's identity have driven him to augment an abnormal religious obsession to the complete withdrawal of a catatonic Christ complex. Imagining himself to be a rock, he reverts to the symbol of castration with which he has destroyed the sacrificial lamb—symbolically, Christ, his father, and himself. It must be acknowledged that, while the above statement permits us to disregard the Oedipus complex, it does not completely rule out the possibility of the importance of this or any other incestuous psychorelationship.

There are many indications of sexual ambivalence in *Miss Lonelyhearts*, not the least of which lies in the irony of the title. That ML has little or no masculine identity is most apparent in his attempt to identify himself over the phone to Fay Doyle:

> "This is Miss Lonelyhearts."
> "Miss who?"
> "Miss Lonelyhearts, Miss Lonelyhearts, the man who does the column."

This ambivalence is completely opposite that of Fay Doyle, for she has written a proposition not to the columnist Miss Lonelyhearts but to a man in a blue suit she had "pointed out" to her at Delehanty's. ML's reaction to Fay's letter is his stock reaction to any woman. Without having seen her, he imagines what she looks like. "He thought of Mrs. Doyle as a tent, hair-covered and veined, and of himself as the skeleton in a water closet, the skull and cross-bones on a scholar's bookplate. When he made the skeleton enter the flesh tent, it flowered at every joint." ML's perverse fantasy portentiously anticipates the relationship he is to share with Fay Doyle, one in which he is to play the feminine part and find "a strange pleasure in having the roles reversed." That he imagines himself as a flowering skeleton extends one of West's most elaborate feminine symbols. Both Freudian and poetic, West uses flowering as an extension of his breast imagery: the magician ML brings dead doorknobs to life by making them flower; Betty's nipples are, to ML, rosebuds which he would like to wear; kissing Mary Shrike, ML's living breast symbol, brings her dead body to life as indicated by her strong artificial flower scent. The pattern of deadness blossoming into femininity is clearly most important, therefore, in this expression of ML's sexual ambivalence.

The theme of sexual ambivalence is also manifested in such minor characters as Miss Farkis and the clean old man. Shrike introduces the theme in the form of a jibe, directly related to ML's sexual identity. With cruel accuracy, he observes: "Oh, so you don't care for women, eh? J. C. is your only sweetheart, eh? Jesus Christ, the King of Kings, the Miss Lonelyhearts of Miss Lonelyhearts. . . .' " Shrike's comment not only emphasizes ML's Christ complex but shades it with apt homosexuality. It is at this time that Miss Farkis enters. "She had long legs, thick ankles, big hands, a powerful body, a slender neck and a childish face made tiny by a man's haircut. . . . She acknowledged the introduction with a masculine handshake." For all her masculinity, Miss Farkis is most appreciated, by Shrike, for her large breasts which, as perceived by ML, are just part of a "powerful body." West's description of Miss Farkis, as a catalogue of what ML's conscious notices, proves even more interesting when compared to the description of Fay Doyle. "Legs like Indian clubs, breasts like balloons and a brow like a pigeon. Despite her short plaid skirt, red sweater, rabbitskin jacket and knitted tam-o'-shanter, she looked like a police captain." The physical masculinity of both women is projected by ML's feelings toward (fear of) them as women. Rather than being a simple condemnation of these "real" people, the descriptions are reflexive, testifying more to ML's sexual ambivalence than to theirs.

George B. Simpson, the clean old man, may be studied in a more sophisticated way. Frightened and hiding in a public men's room near ML's sterile park, the old man asks only to be left alone. His flute-like voice laughs/cries at ML's accusation that he is effeminate, his mind as diseased as his soul. He is a soft lump that cannot protect himself, armed only with a cane and a pair of gloves to protect his hands from redness. Deprived of his phallic cane, Simpson is encouraged to discuss his inversion with ML and his friend. As the old man sticks his tie in his mouth—another sexual allusion—ML is reminded of a frog he had stepped on when a child. Falling into what has become recognized as a behavior pattern, ML's pity and anguish turn to anger, then to violent irrationality as he feels he must destroy the old man.

George Simpson with cane is a forerunner of Peter Doyle. Both represent crippled humanity and both find an identity with ML. ML attempts to adopt his role (consciously Christ, unconsciously homosexual) to make Simpson conform to the now expected (unconsciously sought) role of suffering confidant. In this way, ML enables himself to share the confessor's anguish and displace his own anxiety. In Simpson, ML seeks a passive love-object with whom he can achieve the subconscious role of aggressor, the omnipotent father. ML puts his arm around Simpson and relies on the theatrical pretense of sympathy in his voice to coax the old man. In a curious way, he is repeating the seduction technique he had used with Betty. Like Betty, Simpson remains unmoved and ML turns violent, attacking the humanity he cannot heal—"the sick and miserable, broken and betrayed, inarticulate and impotent." As with Miss Farkis and Fay Doyle, the characterization of Simpson reveals more about ML's perspective and his own character than that of the clean old man. It is interesting to note that in *The Day of the Locust* West created the bizarre Homer Simpson to share the position of protagonist with Tod Hackett. In both novels, it appears that West has used this device of a physically-split personality to enable the main character to converse with the self he does not want to acknowledge. Much in the way Shrike's caustic appraisal of Goldsmith is reflexive, ML's vision of Simpson is a projection of ML as an old man. ML shares the devastating list of qualities which he attributes to humanity as he beats up the old man. ML is compulsively drawn to Simpson because he recognizes himself within the disgusting portrait of the old man's effeminate weakness. Were it not for the fatal intervention of the other cripple, Peter Doyle, ML would all too likely assume an identity similar to Simpson's; however, ML instead will cast off his protective gloves of semi-rationality and be caught red-handed.

Of course, ML's sexual identity climaxes with his relationship to Peter Doyle. Through Doyle, ML is able to break free from the last bonds of rationality. At the Doyle home, ML may now avoid the advances of Fay and smile beautifully in an attempt to recapture the erotic emotion he had experienced when holding Peter's hand. Doyle's sexual identity is further complicated by the role his wife has forced him to play:

> "Ain't I the pimp, to bring home a guy for my wife?" He darted a quick look at Miss Lonelyhearts and laughed apologetically.
>
> Mrs. Doyle was furious. She rolled a newspaper into a club and struck her husband in the mouth with it. He surprised her by playing the fool. He growled like a dog and caught the paper in his teeth. When she let go of her end, he dropped to his hands and knees and then continued the imitation on the floor.
>
> Miss Lonelyhearts tried to get the cripple to stand up and bent to lift him; but, as he did so, Doyle tore open Miss Lonelyhearts' fly, then rolled over on his back, laughing wildly.

The pimping situation mirrors the situation between Mary and Willy Shrike, and ML is again the correspondent. In this case, however, the Doyles fight for the phallus of ML, symbolically represented as a newspaper club. Finally, Doyle's canine pantomime is an acting out of ML's feeble proposition to Mary Shrike: "Sleep with me and I'll be one gay dog." Peter, his very name a crude pun, at length succumbs to a hysterical fit of laughter. The homosexual relationship is so open between Doyle and the Christ-rationalizing ML that the jealous wife later jeers, "What a sweet pair of fairies you guys are." His ambivalence is still indicated when Fay Doyle unsuccessfully attempts to seduce him: "He felt like an empty bottle that is being slowly filled with warm, dirty water." The masculine symbol of the bottle assumes a feminine connotation as it is "violated" by the polluted water West has associated with Fay's gross femininity and with ML's pawnshop hallucination of humanity. Nonetheless, the polar sex roles negate each other in ML's psyche, leaving only the asexual identity of the imperturbable rock.

The destruction of his ego identity is expressed in the fantasy he experiences in a non-dreaming state of delusion. Living on eucharistic crackers and water, ML assumes the identity of a statue holding a stopped clock and a cripple protecting his instrument from the rain. The statue recalls the ivory Christ which he has become in a demented fantasy world beyond time. The rock seems to be a hardened extension of the imagined hump with which he, now one with his sordid humanity, repels the waters of femininity. When a mixed crowd of Shrike's friends breaks into the room, ML makes no attempt to cover his naked body, for he has lost all modesty in his loss of sexual identity.

As Shrike diabolically tempts ML to join their party, ML examines his saltine eucharists, acting out his identity of the rock-Christ. ML agrees to accompany them, for he regards Shrike's taunting as a divine ordeal. With his rock identity, ML believes he can now save crippled humanity because he can now believe the shallow truisms he has been struggling with for so long. More likely, however, he is now totally impotent for, with the rock identity, he has lost even the semblance of compassion. Having forsaken what has appeared to be an existential commitment to humanity, he is now more than ineffectual; he is a threat to the humanity, he is now more than ineffectual; he is a threat to the humanity he would save. Shrike anticipates this in his description of ML's relationship to his readers: " 'You are afraid that even when exposed to his bright flame, you will only smolder and give off a bad smell. Be of good heart, for I know that you will burst into flame. Miss Lonelyhearts is sure to prevail.' " Similar to Shrike's allusion to Attic salt, the metaphor indicates ML's destructive nature, which only ML will survive.

The last chapters of the book reintroduce the complexities of sexual ambiguity, however, as Betty discloses to ML that she is to have his baby and the couple plan their life together. Although ML still regards Betty as a love-object, he no longer wants her to permit him to act out his psychoneurotic anxiety, for he has made real his Christ fantasy with the help of Peter Doyle. But for ML, his sexual identity has not become so much a fruition of latent homosexuality as it has a denial of sexual commitment altogether. It is this new asexual identity which permits ML to play house with Betty at the soda fountain. Robbed of all sexual responses, he feels no threat to his sexuality from his girlfriend. Once aware of the menace of escapism, ML can now accept any dream for he now considers himself beyond experience.

> He did not feel guilt. He did not feel. The rock was a solidification of his feeling, his conscience, his sense of reality, his self-knowledge. He could have planned anything. A castle in Spain and love on a balcony or a pirate trip and love on a tropical island.

When her door closed behind him, he smiled. The rock had been thoroughly tested and had been found perfect.

In Freudian terms, West cites ML's condition not as diagnostic theory but as the conscious "reality" of ML. The vision is itself crippling and a pathetic submission to emotional catatonia, but, as perceived through ML's thoughts, it is a vision of salvation.

Thus it comes to pass that ML embraces his mental breakdown entirely and passionately.

> After a long night and morning, towards noon, Miss Lonelyhearts welcomed the arrival of fever. It promised heat and mentally un-motivated violence. The promise was soon fulfilled; the rock became a furnace.
>
> He fastened his eyes on the Christ that hung on the wall opposite his bed. As he stared at it, it became a bright fly, spinning with quick grace on a background of blood velvet sprinkled with tiny nerve stars.
>
> Everything else in the room was dead. . . .
>
> The room was full of grace. A sweet, clean grace, not washed clean, but clean as the undersides of the inner petals of a newly forced rosebud.
>
> Delight was also in the room. It was like a gentle wind, and his nerves rippled under it like small blue flowers in a pasture.
>
> He was conscious of two rhythms that were slowly becoming one. When they became one, his identification with God was complete. His heart was the one heart, the heart of God. And his brain was likewise God's.
>
> God said, "Will you accept it, now?"
>
> And he replied, "I accept, I accept."

The rosebud grace in ML's fantasy room suggests the essence of Betty as ML again assumes a self-image of flowering. His emotional and intellectual identities do not so much fuse as dissolve into the abyss of his father's identity. ML's psyche achieves an intellectual form of intercourse with his father through total submission of his ego to that of his father-God. West cruelly permits ML to believe he is having a religious experience.

Thus, Doyle's accidental shooting of ML seems not only ironic but justified. In his attempt to escape ML's grasp, his gun, significantly wrapped in a newspaper, goes off unintentionally. Rather than impose any figurative sexual significance upon the incident, we would be wise merely to view the shooting abstractly as a case of self-defense. It may be only assumed that the gun wound is fatal to ML, for the novel ends with no mention of ML's death. This seems only right, for the novel is truly an expression of ML's consciousness.

My purpose so far has been to investigate the main character of *Miss Lonelyhearts*, both contextually and within the Freudian metaphor, with the proper interrelationship between the two approaches as suggested by West himself. We have seen that the most outstanding literary and symptomatic trait in ML's character is his flight into hysterical fantasy. It would appear to manifest itself in the illusionary state of mind which Charcot refers to as *attitudes passionelles* or hallucinations. To corroborate this assumption, we may again look to Freud:

> We say that the dream-wish is converted into an hallucination and as such commands belief in the reality of its fulfillment. . . .
>
> The formation of the wish-phantasy and its regression into hallucination are the most essential parts of the dream-work, but they do not belong exclusively to dreams. On the contrary, they are found similarly in two morbid states: in acute hallucinatory confusion (Meynert's "amentia"), and in the hallucinatory phase of schizophrenia. . . . The hallucinatory phase of schizophrenia has been less thoroughly studied; it seems generally to be of a composite nature, but in its essence it might well correspond to a fresh attempt at restitution, designed to restore to the ideas of objects their libidinal cathexis (*Theory*).

It is with the application of such a key Freudian statement that the relationship between ML's interpretation of his experience and the psychological nature of the character may be more completely defined. Thus, with Freud as our Bulfinch, we are not seeking a new insight on hysteria by our reading of *Miss Lonelyhearts*, but are using psychological theory to aid us in understanding the main character of the work.

The quotation further substantiates the theory that ML's behavior may be comprehended as that of a schizophrenic. Suggested strongly by his latent inversion and ambivalent suspension between subjectified anxiety and rationalized aggression, the condition grows worse as the novel moves from an openly obsessional neurosis to hysterical catatonia.

Within the literary framework of *Miss Lonelyhearts*, West has provided us with a character whose thinking is not only "complex, overabstract, and autistic" as symptomatic of his schizoid personality, but he has done so within the confines of the narrative form. By definition, the main character will appear complex and autistic as we devote our attention to studying his personality, and the overabstractions are so fundamental to the contextual unity of the narrative that we do not recognize the full significance of their intensity at first reading. From the beginning of the book, ML's hostility and subsequent frustration are made evident, and it is clear that, with the exception of ML's tryst with Betty in the country, his interpersonal relationships have only served to augment this feeling of alienation.

We have seen how the theme of ML's inability to experience genuine emotion, gradually extended as his rock identity, is suggested from the beginning of the novel. ML's fantasy is that he would imagine himself a Christ, a martyr of the unintelligible masses who write to him. However, he is actually a perverse extension of his alter ego, Shrike, in that he uses the suffering of his readers to gratify his fantasies. He laments that he must try to answer the irresolvable problems of his readers, but when the clean old man refuses to accept the role of supplicant, ML reacts with a literal fit of rage. Although ML at first appears to represent an existential prototype, painfully and passionately aware of the futility of the human condition, this, we have seen, is merely a mask for the Christ fantasy. ML's relationship to the existential predicament transcends commitment; indeed, it turns upon itself. ML uses the human condition as a vehicle for his masochistic play, finds suffering to be a play thing—a drama of guilt and torture in which he can star, performing with self-consciously obvious gestures, with Betty, Mary Shrike, and finally Peter Doyle. Almost in the sexual sense, ML permits—forces—himself to be violated by the misery of his readers. Such a manipulation of role-playing affords him a passive self-image of compassion. The ultimate signifiance, however, lies in the fact that, when denied this role by Betty or Simpson, ML will do his best to create such a situation. It is only within the blind limits of his own perversion that ML can experience anything whatsoever.

The disintegration of ML's thought processes have been most notable in his surreal dreams and semi-fantasies, again culminating in the rock-Christ. In accordance with the definition provided by Coville, the new identity may be seen to have some elements of both hallucination and delusion. Relating to ML's malady, it would seem more strongly allied to the concept of a delusion (of grandeur), whereas the attacks of hysteria complement the definition of visual hallucinations.

Up to the point at which ML meets Peter Doyle, his condition closely resembles that referred to as "simple schizophrenic reaction."

> The outstanding symptoms are a gradual narrowing of interests, loss of ambition, emotional apathy, and withdrawal from social relations. Personal appearance is neglected, conversation is meager, and there is indifference to the opposite sex. The patient appears

to be completely absorbed in his inner world of fantasy. . . . Close observation of such individuals often uncovers weak, distorted efforts to make contact with others, as a consequence of the pathetic need for love and affection which these patients experience. Usually, however, it is not possible to maintain any emotional contact with them.

ML's obsession with the anxiety-ridden, anxiety-inflicting letters reflects his narrowing of interests and serves as a major reason for his inability to work after his return from the country. ML makes three short calls on the city room during the novel but never finishes a reply to a letter satisfactorily, that we may read. The outstanding symptoms are equally apparent when the party crowd invade his room in the last section of the novel; however, ML's delusion, through its isolationism, assumes elements of a catatonic reaction:

> In the stuporous state, the patient loses all animation, remaining motionless and in a stereotyped posture for hours, even days. He refuses food and shows no effort to control bowels or bladder. Extreme negativism is a characteristic reaction. . . . Hallucinations and delusions occur in this stuporous state, and they may involve the patient in a conflict of cosmic significance (for example, the forces of Good and Evil may be experienced as at mortal combat in his body). The stereotyped posture and gestures are frequently related symbolically to the patient's fantasy experience.

Clearly, ML never reaches the full catatonic stupor in which his body would be frozen in a single position—except at the most extreme states of hysteria.

I have used clinical psychology to explain the nature of ML's behavior; the only task remaining is to discern the cause of his derangement.

Especially relevant to the analysis of *Miss Lonelyhearts* is Freud's definition of "obsessional neurosis":

> Here we are at first in doubt what it is that we have to regard as the repressed instinct-presentation—a libidinal or a hostile trend. This uncertainty arises because the obsessional neurosis rests on the premise of a regression by means of which a sadistic trend has been substituted for a tender one. It is this hostile impulse against a loved person which has undergone repression. The effect at an early phase of the work of regression is quite different from that produced later. At first the regression is completely successful, the ideational content is rejected and the effect made to

disappear. As a substitute-formation there arises an alteration in
the ego, an increased sensitiveness of conscience, which can hardly be called a symptom. Substitute—and symptom-formation do
not coincide here. Here, too, we learn something about the
mechanism of repression. Repression, as it invariably does, has
brought about a withdrawal of libido, but for this purpose it has
made use of a "reaction-formation", by intensifying an
antithesis. . . .

But the repression, at first successful, does not hold; in the further course of things its failure becomes increasingly obvious. The
ambivalence which has allowed repression to come into being by
means of reaction-formation also constitutes the point at which
the repressed succeeds in breaking through again. The vanished
effect is transformed without any diminuation, into dread of the
community, pangs of conscience, or self-reproaches; the rejected
idea is replaced by a displacement-substitute.

Within these concepts, Freud provides a rationale for the action of the novel.
More pertinent, however, is the way in which the observation relates to the
source of ML's trouble.

Freud devotes an entire essay to the relationship between obsessions and
religious inclinations, in which he finds several parallels between the strong
emotional affinity some people draw from a religion and the emotional
character of a psychoneurotic. Not only does his investigation uncover
similarities in emotional states but in origin as well:

The structure of a religion seems also to be founded on the sup-
pression or renunciation of certain instinctual trends; these trends
are not, however, as in neurosis, exclusively components of the
sexual instincts, though even these, for the most part, are not
without sexual element. The sense of guilt in consequence of continual temptation, and the anxious expectation in the guise of fear
of divine punishment, have indeed been familiar to us in religion
longer than in neurosis.

It seems in perfect accord with the general outline of West's novel that the
main character's psychoreligious problems may be better understood in the
light of these theories.

It has been an accepted tenet of this essay that ML's religious obsession
is closely linked with his relationship to his father. As viewed through the
lamb sacrifice, ML assumes his father's role of priest and attempts to express
his castration anxiety at the bungled ritual. Again we reaffirm our conclu-

sion that ML's schizophrenia is a manifestation of childhood neuroses of castration and incest complexes.

Just what exactly is known to us about ML's childhood? We know that his father was a Baptist minister and raised his family in the tradition of New England puritanism. We know that ML had a sister four years younger than himself and are told of his fascination at playing the piano while she danced. While in college, ML, by then an agnostic, symbolically crushed his (perhaps ambivalently his father's) head with a rock. At the book's close, ML is again a priest of sacrifice in the psychopathic identity of the rock. There is, as Reid has mentioned, nothing said about ML's mother. It is possible to go outside contextual bounds and suggests that ML's memory of his mother is so guilt-laden that he has suppressed it completely from his conscious, but such a projection is neither fair nor necessary.

Of more revealing interest is the relationship between ML and his younger sister. Drinking at the speakeasy, ML experiences a heightening of sensual awareness and paranoia which subsides into childhood memory:

> He forgot that his heart was a bomb to remember an incident of his childhood. One winter evening, he had been waiting with his little sister for their father to come home from church. She was eight years old then, and he was twelve. Made sad by the pause between playing and eating, he had gone to the piano and had begun a piece by Mozart. It was the first time he had ever voluntarily gone to the piano. His sister left her picture book to dance to his music. She had never danced before. She danced gravely and carefully, a simple dance yet formal. . . . As Miss Lonelyhearts stood at the bar, swaying slightly to the remembered music, he thought of children dancing. Square replacing oblong being replaced by circle. Every child, everywhere; in the whole world there was not one child who was not gravely, sweetly dancing.

Enigmatically, it is the only scene in the novel which is pure, free from sordid suffering, or even completely pleasant. Alone with his sister and conscious of his father's temporary absence, the boy finds delight in the simple act shared by him and his sister. As dream symbols, dancing and playing piano are equated with orgasm in countless Freud articles. West has further stressed the concept of initiation, for it is a new experience for both youngsters. Nor is it coincidental that the young ML is experiencing this symbolic coitus at the age of puberty. His tendency to elaborate the incident into an abstract situation, one in which all the children in the world participate, links the innocent memory to ML's current schizoid condition. His sister's dance further accounts for ML's obsession with order while the father's absence introduces the theme of subconscious sexual rivalry.

Those who question the sister's place in the incestuous picture should again look to Freud:

> All that I have been able to add to our understanding of it [the horror of incest] is to emphasize the fact that it is essentially an *infantile* feature and that it reveals a striking agreement with the mental life of neurotic patients. Psychoanalysis has taught us that a boy's earliest choice of objects for his love is incestuous and that those objects are forbidden ones—his mother and his sister. We have learnt, too, the manner in which, as he grows up, he liberates himself from this incestuous attraction. A neurotic, on the other hand, invariably exhibits some degree of psychical infantilism. He has either failed to get free from the psychosexual conditions that prevailed in his childhood or he has returned to them—two possibilities which may be summed up as developmental inhibition and regression. Thus incestuous fixations of the libido continue to play (or begin once more to play) the principle part in his unconscious mental life. We have arrived at the point of regarding a child's relation to his parents, dominated as it is by incestuous longings, as the nuclear complex of neurosis.

Despite Hyman's attempt to link ML's neurosis to the best-known incest relationship, the context of the novel obviously negates the Oedipal influence in its affirmation of the more dominant brother-sister relationship.

As ML's incestuous desire for his sister contributes the basis for his neurotic inversion, it also resolves the dilemma of defining Betty's importance in the novel. With thumb-like breasts contributing to her boyish (and, more significantly, child-like) physique, ML sees his sister in Betty. Having relived the terrifying castration ritual, he seeks the order he has associated with his sister's dance and goes to Betty for comfort. But being confronted by the love-object he would repress, he is overcome with a renewed guilt and anxiety. Sado-masochistically, he attempts to force her to punish him— thereby fulfilling his tormented guilt feelings, and, with ambiguous gestures of eroticism, making her share in his uncomprehending frustration. When she asks him to leave, he goes to Delehanty's where the memory of "innocent" love is recalled, momentarily purged of incestuous guilt. Picking up the old homosexual, ML again feels guilty and he releases his hostility on a projection of himself through George Simpson.

Disgusted by Simpson, ML remembers another childhood experience:

"Miss Lonelyhearts felt as he had felt years before when he had accidentally stepped on a small frog. Its spilled guts had filled him with pity, but when its suffering had become real to his senses, his pity had turned to rage and he had beaten it frantically until it was dead." As we have already seen, the incident is in keeping with the pattern set by ML's other outbursts of hysterical violence. It is through such a recalled instance that humanity (Simpson) becomes a part of the castration rite, thus assuming a similar role in the guilt pattern associated with the Christ complex. Returning to Freud's catalogue of dream symbols, however, reveals a more subtle implication. "Children and brothers and sisters," Freud observes, "are less tenderly treated, being symbolized by *little animals* or *vermin*." Guilt feelings towards ML's sister are symbolized here in such a way that ML, the aggressor, is the inflictor of pain. Unable to cope with the emotion (a mixture of incestuous desire and guilt) and incapable of tolerating the real experience of pain, he obliterates the problem much in the way he attempted to remove the threat of his father (as the lamb). Now feeling guilt about his own actions, he turns on himself through Simpson. The description of the incident is further a key to the final fate of ML, for it allegorically testifies to the perverse manner in which he perceives and interprets the suffering of others.

"Miss Lonelyhearts in the Country" appears less mystifying once Betty's sister role has been accepted. Initially, ML refrains from aggressive sexplay with Betty out of alleged respect for her virginity. However, when ML sees Betty's naked, child-like body as she hangs out laundry on the line, he is sexually aroused for a "normal" heterosexual union. "He blew her a kiss. She caught it with a gesture that was childishly sexual. He vaulted the porch rail and ran to kiss her. As they went down, he smelled a mixture of sweat, soap and crushed grass." Inspired by her "childishly sexual" gesture, ML unconsciously makes love not to Betty, but to his sister. Incidentally, it is this same childish naivete which arouses ML on his date with Mary Shrike. ML has been kneading her body passionlessly until he seems suddenly aroused as she recites the morbid saga of her mother's death "in a brave voice, like a little girl reciting at a party."

The little girl at a party is an image which recurs at the end of the novel as the description of Betty. On the surface, the image could hardly appear less appropriate, for Betty has just told ML that she is pregnant. However, it is especially apt as an extension of ML's consciousness, for ML, now fully immured in his rock identity, need no longer acknowledge Betty's "real" identity. To him, she has lost all actual existence except as a little girl's party dress. Attracted to the adolescent frilliness that is associated with what West calls "her little-girl-in-the-party-dress air," ML begs the dress, not Betty, to marry him. He is so protected from "reality" by his own rock identity that he can seriously contemplate marriage so long as the two of them play as children at a soda fountain—like brother and sister playing house. The irony that this asexual relationship is actually the fruition of ML's sexual repression is coupled with the irony that their psychological roles have been reversed: while Betty had once been the symbol of stability for the vicious ML, ML now regards himself as the embodiment of stability for the irritable and frightened (due to her pregnancy) Betty. Without the incestuous motivation for their affair, Betty's announcement that she is going to have a baby would remain in conflict with the homosexual theme of the novel and seem unnecessary melodrama.

Betty is, for ML, his sister. By the time he has established communications with God and won approval from this psychic-father, the psychic-son of God is prepared for the corrupted miracle of rebirth. It is only fitting that Betty should be present at the miracle, for it is because of her that Peter does not turn back. Psychologically, and physically, she is the barrier which brings about ML's destruction.

The Problem of Language in *Miss Lonelyhearts*

Jeffrey L. Duncan

Almost halfway through his story Miss Lonelyhearts gets sick. His sickness is essentially spiritual—he is, the chapter title says, "in the Dismal Swamp"— and it has been brought on by his job. His girlfriend, Betty, brings him some hot soup and advice: quit, try another line of work. He tells her that quitting would not help much because he would still remember the letters. She does not understand, so he offers her an explanation of unusual length and formality:

> Perhaps I can make you understand. Let's start from the beginning. A man is hired to give advice to the readers of a newspaper. The job is a circulation stunt and the whole staff considers it a joke. He welcomes the job, for it might lead to a gossip column, and anyway he's tired of being a leg man. He too considers the job a joke, but after several months at it, the joke begins to escape him. He sees that the majority of the letters are profoundly humble pleas for moral and spiritual advice, that they are inarticulate expressions of genuine suffering. He also discovers that his correspondents take him seriously. For the first time in his life, he is forced to examine the values by which he lives. This examination shows him that he is the victim of the joke and not its perpetrator.

Here he stops, satisfied it seems that there is no more to say. Betty still does not understand, to no one's surprise, but we do: Miss Lonelyhearts cannot answer the letters because he has found that his values do not, cannot, justify genuine suffering, including his own. (For he is suffering too, languishing

From *The Iowa Review* 8, no. 1 (Winter 1977). © 1977 by the University of Iowa.

in the dismal swamp.) Hence he is the victim of the joke: the advice-giver is himself sick-of-it-all, in desperate need of advice.

He does not say what his values are (or were), but he does not really need to. He has found them, he implies, not just wanting, but false. His crisis then is intensely personal, because *he* has been false, and still is. He no longer claims a proper name, and he wears at all times his workaday nom de plume, a woman's at that. But not only is he no lady, he cannot fulfill the requirements, as he construes them, that his pseudonym entails. He has become a misnomer. In one sense, though, the name suits him: he is as lonely a heart as any of his correspondents. Accordingly, the only identity he feels entitled to is the same one they assume, the victim. Better any identity than none, we might say, but not so. For he has come to doubt all values and therefore the value of suffering itself. If it has no value, neither does the role of victim. One simply suffers, that's all, without upshot or significance, the butt of a joke.

What makes the joke *bad* is the fact, as Miss Lonelyhearts sees it, that the suffering his correspondents express is genuine. Others have agreed. In his review of the novel, for instance, William Carlos Williams protested, "The letters which West uses freely and at length must be authentic. I can't believe anything else. The unsuspected world they reveal is beyond ordinary thought." Thirty some years later Randall Reid said the same thing: "They [the letters] have the vividness and the unarguable reality of a revelation." Both statements, cueing off Miss Lonelyhearts, couple authenticity and revelation. The letters reveal a reality that is unarguable. They are, like revelation, their own evidence. Upon seeing them one believes them, if not instantaneously, like Williams, then slowly, gradually like Miss Lonelyhearts. Their truth, in other words, is not a matter of fact, but an article of faith, and no one has questioned it. I think we should, just as I think that, deep down, Miss Lonelyhearts himself does. At issue is a central concern, the nature of language, both as a theme and as the medium of West's novel.

Miss Lonelyhearts deals primarily not with people, but with letters, with various orders and disorders of words. In his personal relations he is not engaged in dialogue, the language of spontaneous give and take, nearly so much as he is confronted with speeches, with words as deliberately composed as those of the letters, if not more so. Notably, in the two days (and chapters) before he beds himself in the dismal swamp, he hears two speeches, one by Mary Shrike, then one by Fay Doyle, that amount to letters in the flesh. "People like Mary were unable to do without such tales. They told them because they wanted to talk about something besides clothing or business or the movies, because they wanted to talk about something poetic." Like Mary like Fay:

they simply have different poetics. Understandably Miss Lonelyhearts listens to neither. They reveal a reality, unarguably, but it is hardly one of genuine suffering, much less of profound humility. Instead they betray mere attitudes struck, postures assumed, poses wantonly displayed, a comic pornography of suffering and trouble. If they express anything authentic—though it is doubtful that these women give a fig about authenticity—it is a desire for suffering, for indisputable reality, personal significance. And if they are to be pitied, it is because they do not, perhaps cannot, suffer.

That is, they have nothing really to speak of, Mary and Fay. Their words merely fill in their blanks. And what is true of them may also—since West's characters are consistently thin—be true of the others, of Betty, of Desperate, of Broad Shoulders, of Shrike, of Miss Lonelyhearts himself. For that reason, if no other, Shrike can burlesque the letters, the expressions of undeserved, unmitigated suffering, just as effectively as he can parody the conventional formulae of value, of the life worth living:

> This one is a jim-dandy. A young boy wants a violin. It looks simple; all you have to do is get the kid one. But then you discover that he has dictated the letter to his little sister. He is paralyzed and can't even feed himself. He has a toy violin and hugs it to his chest, imitating the sound of playing with his mouth. How pathetic! However, one can learn much from this parable. Label the boy Labor, the violin Capital, and so on.

> So you buy a farm and walk behind your horse's moist behind, no collar or tie, plowing your broad swift acres. As you turn up the rich black soil, the wind carries the smell of pine and dung across the fields and the rhythm of an old, old work enters your soul. To this rhythm, you sow and weep and chivy your kine, not kin or kind, between the pregnant rows of corn and taters.

Shrike can handle them with equal facility because he insists that they bear the same message, and that it is their only message: the human race is a poet that writes the eccentric propositions of its fate, and propositions, fate, the race itself amount only to so much noisy breath, hot air, flatulence.

Miss Lonelyhearts reluctantly suspects as much. That is why he can find no sincere answers, why he can take nothing he says or thinks seriously, why he lacks the courage of his clichés, why he converts even an original formulation immediately into a cliché. "Man has a tropism for order," he thinks to himself; "The physical world has a tropism for disorder, entropy. Man against Nature . . . the battle of the centuries." A capital "N" no less.

Four sentences later he dismisses it for good: "All order is doomed, yet the battle is worthwhile." No wonder then that only a little while later he casts his explanation to Betty in the third person—it accommodates exactly his ironic self-consciousness, the distance between what he wants to believe and what he suspects. No wonder as well that his explanation sounds like another speech, one that he has often rehearsed to himself; it is so pat, so articulate, the cool, collected rhetoric of desperation, of futile resolves, private last-stands. For if he can only bring himself to believe what he says, that the suffering is genuine, he may yet hope to believe that it can be justified. That is, faith, once succumbed to, may wax and multiply like irony succumbed to. But the "if" is difficult; it requires breaking the force of irony, which is considerable. Not only can it move mountains, it can annihilate them. And people, too.

Irony is not always humorous, but humor is always ironic. And the letters in the book are humorous.

> I am in such pain I dont know what to do sometimes I think I will kill myself my kidneys hurt so much. . . . I was operatored on twice and my husband promised no more children on the doctors advice as he said I might die but when I got back from the hospital he broke his promise and now I am going to have a baby and I don't think I can stand it my kidneys hurt so much.

The writers have had nothing to do with the terrible turns their fates have taken—they are innocent—and neither they nor anyone else can do a thing about their difficulties. Their problems are, by their own terms, insoluble; they themselves are, by their own accounts, schlmiels with Weltschmerz; "I don't know what to do," concludes Sick-of-it-all. "Ought I commit suicide?" queries Desperate. "What is the whole stinking business for?" muses Peter Doyle. They are actually seeking confirmation, not advice; they want someone else to see them as they see themselves. Also the letters are all graced by the common touch, illiteracy. The writers seem sublimely unaware that their words, like double agents, constantly betray them. "But he [Broad Shoulders's boarder] tries to make me bad and as there is nobody in the house when he comes home drunk on Saturday night I dont know what to do but so far I didnt let him." Betrayal is revelation, but of a fundamentally ambiguous sort: we cannot say whether the words of the letters misrepresent or faithfully execute their authors as they really are. Either way, though, they are funny. The slip of the tongue, Freudian or otherwise, reliably gets a laugh.

Miss Lonelyhearts, however, no longer finds the letters funny because he assumes they are authentic. Genuine suffering, he tells Betty, is no joke. This difference between his response and ours gets us at last into the troubled heart of the novel. Suffering is not funny, certainly, but it has been since Eden, no less than vanity and folly, the very stuff of humor. Pathos, too, of course, and tragedy, but we pay for the loss of Paradise with laughter as well as tears, and comedy is one of the more common forms of man's inhumanity to man. But nothing is more human, for we are considering one application of our capacity for abstraction, our ability to translate instances of suffering and pain into symbol systems that go absurdly awry. Humor is a function of symbolic consciousness. It involves the displacement if not the annihilation of persons, their particular reality, by words, a particular scheme of concepts. The unnamed perpetrator of the joke is language, like West's, for example, when he describes the letters as all alike, "stamped from the dough of suffering with a heart-shaped cookie knife." Just as West's words undercut the letters, so the letters' words displace their writers: "it dont pay to be inocent and is only a big disapointment." Miss Lonelyhearts no longer finds the letters funny because he refuses to consent to this displacement, to bless this annihilation with a laugh. He looks over or through their words to their writers, as he imagines them: profoundly humble, genuinely suffering, terribly real.

But Shrike recognizes a laugh when he sees one, and Miss Lonelyhearts knows it. That is why he has to insist that the letters are not funny: they are not because in truth they are, and that, in his opinion, is wrong, all wrong. For it is not just the letters—he doesn't find anything funny. He will not be a party to humor per se, and therefore, consistently enough, he tries to leave the premises of language altogether, in violence, in women's flesh, in a rural retreat, and in a hand-holding soul-session in a speakeasy.

His expeditions fail, hardly to his surprise, because in them he only finds himself engaged face-to-face with more words on the loose. Sometimes they are spoken, sometimes they are enacted, but they are always there, inescapable. "With the return of self-consciousness, he knew that only violence could make him supple." Spiritually speaking, I take it. His violence serves a metaphysical cause self-consciously conceived. Instead of delivering him from language into whatever—say reality—it necessarily forces him into obeisance to language. For language is its maker. He works over the clean old man for his story, the dubious words of his life—"Yes, I know, your tale is a sad one. Tell it, damn you, tell it"—and sees him at last as the embodiment of his correspondents, his letters. Mary gives him a little of her body to tell him all of her tale; Fay uses her story as a pretext for sex, but she also uses sex as a pretext for her story. Betty believes in a *Sunset* version of *Walden*, and for a while Miss Lonelyhearts is able to relax in her belief, but when they get back to the city he realizes that "he had begun to think himself a faker and a fool." So he is back in language again, and not at all sure that he ever really left it. Like violence, his session of silence with Doyle serves a metaphysical purpose self-consciously forced to its crisis: "He . . . drove his hand back and forced it to clasp the cripple's . . . pressed it firmly with all the love he could manage." This may be a flight of the alone to the alone, but the wings are words, words like "love" and "communion," like "together" and "alone." His only real hope, then, as he has seen it all along, is Christ, appropriately enough.

Let us go back to the dismal swamp. "He was thinking of how Shrike had accelerated his sickness by teaching him to handle his one escape, Christ, with a thick glove of words." Shrike does not get his entire due: he has taught Miss Lonelyhearts to handle everything with a thick glove of words, to suspect that there may be nothing really for the glove to handle, nothing for it to do but make figures of itself, or that the glove, like a magician's white one, renders whatever reality it handles null and void. Genuine magic, though, not legerdemain. Destructive force. The word "escape," in this context, usually means a flight from reality to some more tenable opposite. In Miss Lonelyhearts's case, however, it seems to mean a flight from words in and of themselves to that only (as he sees it) which can redeem them, put them in their proper place—a flight from the terrible logic of Shrike to the Logos itself, Christ, the Word made flesh. The Word informs flesh, flesh substantiates the Word: reality then carries a life-time guarantee, its value insured by language. Then tropes can become unironic Truth, victims can become martyrs, and Paradise, that place of complete integration, can be regained.

Or so a Christian might have it: not an escape, like Tahiti, the soil, hedonism, or art, but a redemption. West's script, however, follows the Christian's with a thumb on its nose and its fingers sadly crossed. Peter Doyle's letter moves Miss Lonelyhearts to holding hands. Later, though, Doyle's hearthside demeanor bankrupts the credibility of his prose, so much that Miss Lonelyhearts takes himself to bed. This time, however, instead of languishing in despair, he becomes the rock. In that metaphor of the Church he has finally, he solipsistically thinks, found himself. "The rock was a solidification of his feeling, his conscience, his sense of reality, his self-knowledge." Thus solidified, though, he feels nothing, and nothing (except the rock) seems real. Betty is a party dress to whom he can say anything without deliberately lying because there is no one to lie to and nothing to lie about. "He could have planned anything. A castle in Spain and love on a balcony or a pirate trip and love on a tropical island." He has changed the game from show-and-tell to play-pretend. As a preliminary to his union with Christ he seems to have gained himself by renouncing words and the world, as he had apparently hoped. But he has actually done nothing of the sort: Miss Lonelyhearts, a pseudonym, has merely become a metaphor, the rock, in a world that was never his.

Up to this point he has always been afraid of Christ. "As a boy in his father's church, he had discovered that something stirred in him when he shouted the name of Christ, something secret and enormously powerful." Later he construes this thing in clinical terms, as hysteria, though he wishes he could believe that it is more than that, that it is actual divinity. Whatever it actually is, his fear is the traditional one of self-relinquishment, of letting go. But now that he has such a definitive sense of self—a rock is definite, if nothing else—he is ironically no longer afraid, and silently shouting the name Christ to himself, he gives himself up and over and has his union. "Christ is life and light." He is also love and Miss Lonelyhearts's new feature editor.

He is, in other words, yet another metaphor, a whole string of them—not the Word, but a word, signifying neither more nor less than any other. Nothing is redeemed, least of all language. Doyle arrives, bad poetry on a field rampant. He has come in the name of secular romantic love to avenge Miss Lonelyhearts's alleged insult to his wife's honor. The allegation is hers, of course, and it is as false as her honor, as her husband's love, as his mission's motive. Miss Lonelyhearts sees him as a sign and, mistaking his warning for a humble plea, goes in the name of divine love to perform a literal miracle, to save Doyle, to save all his correspondents in Doyle's figure, just as he had sought to hurt them all in the figure of the clean old man. Doyle loses heart, so to speak, and tries to flee. Betty, the idle figure of Miss Lonelyhearts's secular fancy, blunders in. Doyle's gun accidentally goes off, and Miss Lonelyhearts meets his end at last, not as martyr, but as unwitting victim, and not as victim of "reality" but of a symbol system gone absurdly awry—of a joke, if you will—because there is no other way for it to go. There is no truth for Miss Lonelyhearts, only words.

It may seem then that Shrike has the last word. All we really have, all we really are, says Shrike, is words, but he does not stop there. There is no cause for grief, he consistently implies, only occasion for jokes. Jokes are his form of prophecy, and they are self-fulfilling. Their form is their content, for their only point is the perfect pointlessness of it all. Nothing is wrong because nothing ever was or could be right. Nothing really matters, not even the fact that nothing really matters. This second step, though, Shrike follows by choice, not of logical necessity. He pronounces "truth" only in order to evade it, to protect himself from pain. Between nothing and grief he will take nothing, not because it is true, finally, but because it is easier.

But while Shrike may take this second step for the sake of comfort, one could argue that the novel takes it of necessity. In open concord with Shrike, it depicts language as radically false, a fundamentally misleading order of being, or nonbeing, as the case may be. Yet the novel is itself a form of language. It would seem then that either the theme must render the form futile, a design of dumb noise, or the form must render the theme gratuitous. But if the theme is gratuitous, the form is perforce futile: it is predicated on counterfeit, a phony issue. Either way (or both ways?) the novel would amount to a display in negation, like the self-dismantling sculpture of Tinguely, like the jokes of Shrike. But Shrike is good only for a laugh, whereas the last elaborate joke of the novel occasions dismay. That is, we respond as if both the statement and the structure were ontologically sound. Now it could be that West has misled us to the very end, that we, to the extent that we care about the outcome, are the unwitting butts of his joke and he is snickering up his sleeve. If so, then West's novel would seem to give us the void as a stripper, taking it all off. On the other hand, our response may be warranted. Curiously enough, we have the same problem with the book that Miss Lonelyhearts has with the letters: whatever we finally deem it, we are necessarily engaged in an act of faith. But we need not, as a consequence, simply toss the book up for grabs.

For the sake of his faith, Miss Lonelyhearts must ignore the bad language of the letters. We enjoy the same language because it is so good: "I bought a new sowing machine as I do some sowing for other people to make both ends meet. . . ." The paradox is simple yet profound. All of the demonstrations of bad language—the letters, Miss Lonelyhearts's awful answers, Shrike's parodies—all involve not only an exhibition of West's skill, but of the adequacy of language to his skill. In order to make humorous "nonsense" (as in the quote just cited), language must be able to make common sense. Further, it must make both kinds at once, since it is precisely the play of the one off the other that is funny. A joke reveals the meaningfulness of language. And like revelation, it constitutes its own evidence: the simple fact that it is funny, that *we* laugh, makes the case.

Now we can understand why Shrike is such a desperate character, insistent, shrill. He cannot make his point—the meaninglessness of it *all*—without contradicting himself. Jokes are his form of prophecy, and they betray him every time. He is the victim of his own success. He grieves, in his fashion, that he cannot have nothing.

But the fact that language is meaningful does not necessarily mean that it is significant, any more than a correct sentence is necessarily true. A philosophical idealist might disagree, of course, but West's characters are not idealists. They want some words that signify something beyond their own sound and sense, something, preferably a redemptive Absolute, that can be empirically ascertained. Miss Lonelyhearts, for example, has no quarrel with the coherence of Betty's "world view," but with its significance. Her order, as far as he is concerned, does not match reality—they are an odd pair—whereas his own disorder does. His experience tells him so, or so he thinks. However, we cannot say whether his confusion results from or produces the confusion he perceives, nor whether the world he perceives is in fact a disorder. For it is not the relation between words and reality that West depicts, it is the disjunction: his characters cannot find out what, if anything, lies on the other side of their words. As a bridge, language breaks; as a window, it shuts out, like stained glass, and keeps his characters in. But it does not become genuinely false, actually misleading, until West's characters believe the bridge is sound, the window perfectly transparent, their words reliably significant, true. As, for instance, when Shrike insists there is nought beyond, and when Miss Lonelyhearts insists there is confusion, or Christ, the Word intact. They do not know, literally, what they are talking about.

Words in the novel fail to do the job West's characters assign them—to reveal a reality beyond themselves. But at the same time the words of the novel, West's words, manage quite successfully to do their job, to reveal all they need to, the patterns their sound and sense make: "the gray sky looked as if it had been rubbed with a soiled eraser. It held no angels, flaming crosses, olive-bearing doves, wheels within wheels. Only a newspaper struggled in the air like a kite with a broken spine." These words do not match reality, fit any empirical facts. Neither do they distort any facts or displace reality. They are not *about* something beyond themselves, an actual person's experience, a historical event. They constitute, rather, their own reality, and their only job is to be true to the structure of which they are a part, that is, to be right, self-consistent, aesthetically correct. Were it some other character than Miss Lonelyhearts sitting there, the sky might very properly contain angels, crosses, doves, wheels, a cloud that speaks, a breeze that inspires, a pulse that beats. In art, language is free of obligation to referents; it is free to be strictly itself, and it stands or falls entirely on its own. And when it stands, it satisfies the idealist and the empiricist alike, for it is simultaneously as conceptual as any law and as phenomenal as an apple falling. It is completely sensible. The poet, as Emerson happily put it, "adorns nature with a new thing."

Our relationship with the novel, then, is not exactly analogous to Miss Lonelyhearts's with the letters. The language of each (even when it is the same) draws different duty. For that reason, the demonstrable error of his and his companions' way does not necessarily compromise the validity of ours.

We place our bets on a different thing, and we have demonstrably good grounds for our wager, namely, the novel's coherence. Being or non-being, it is an *order* of experience. Thus the novel's theme does not necessarily undermine its form. Still, we must recognize that the center of the analogy holds: the novel's coherence depends upon our faith. The world seems able to survive capricious gods, but a work of fiction cannot survive an unreliable third-person narrator. (First-person narrators are a different story, of course, but their implied third-person narrators are not.) Try to imagine, for instance, the last passage I quoted as misleading, false, the sky as actually blue, bearing crosses, wheels, and so forth. The whole show stops; all bets are off. But we in fact read on because we trust the narrator. In order to read on, we must. And in reading on we find constant justification of our faith: the novel elaborates its problem without sentimental dodges or cheap solutions. True to itself, it is true to us. As for those novels that self-consciously make even their third-person reliability suspect, our willing suspension of belief amounts to a working agreement based on the same trust, that they will prove to be meaningful orders of experience. But by meaningful I do not want to suggest comfortable or reassuring. On the contrary, almost all art worth the name repays our faith by raising hell within us, with our cherished assumptions and secret illusions, with our workaday values and beliefs. For it takes us as far as words can go, and thus brings us face-to-face, finally, with silence, mystery. "Emotion" comes from *emovere*, "to move out of," "disturb." Let us momentarily suppose that West has conned us at the end. Now that we are on to it, we can easily dismiss the book, for he has given us the void *merely* as a stripper, a tease, not a real threat but a pretence of one. "Ah," we can say in relief, "he didn't mean it after all."

But West's novel does disturb us, threaten, because its form makes its theme intensely meaningful, utterly real. Here we witness words falling short of reality, and here, and here, and we watch their continual shortcomings compose an actual pattern of doom. We are unsettled because most of us are, like Dr. Johnson, rock-kickers—we ordinarily assume that our words signify something beyond themselves—and reading this story forces us to face the possibility that they do not. The story defines the issue that has become major in certain circles, "the problem of language." But West simultaneously solves the problem *in* the form, every word of the way. For unlike his characters, malpracticing empiricists all, and unlike most of us, West was, as an artist, a practicing idealist. We know that he got the idea for his novel from seeing actual letters to an advice columnist. Had he been concerned with historical-empirical fidelity, he could have used them more-or-less intact. But we also know that he changed them radically, that he in truth wrote his own letters, to make them right, aesthetically correct. All artists, of course, change things to suit their purposes, but their purposes have a single premise, that the work of art must be absolutely true to itself, self-integral, one. Then it can stand and unfold itself, an articulated body of ideas, an avatar of Being.

The novel is an order of being, finally, because in it West shows us that words realize our possibilities as well as define our limits. Miss Lonelyhearts looks at a gray sky and, empiricist that he is, sees only a dirty *tabula rasa*. Against that he sees the most referential and hence ephemeral of all literature, a newspaper, failing (naturally) to soar. But West's words lift nicely, bearing for the space of our imagination all the significance Miss Lonelyhearts misses in his, not in the form of crosses and doves, to be sure, but in the form of figures, of ideas, of words touched with life and touching us with the same.

West's other three stories suffer to varying degrees in comparison with *Miss Lonelyhearts*. They demonstrate a precise but simplistic satire, a sentimental obsession with easy pickings: in *The Dream Life of Balso Snell,* the contrived labyrinths of literary journeys, in *A Cool Million,* the Horatio Alger myth, in *The Day of the Locust,* the Hollywood motif. The unreality of West's marks is patent, their exposure therefore, funny or not, perfunctory: "The fat lady in the yachting cap was going shopping, not boating; the man in the Norfolk jacket and Tyrolean hat was returning, not from a mountain, but an insurance office. . . ." They expose bills of fraudulent goods that we, his readers, declined to buy in the first place; hence they do not disturb, they merely confirm our glib assumptions. *Miss Lonelyhearts*, on the other hand, makes us reconsider.

Here is the difference I mean:

> It is hard to laugh at the need for beauty and romance, no matter how tasteless, even horrible, the results of that need are. But it is easy to sigh. Few thing are sadder than the truly monstrous.
>
> *(The Day of the Locust)*

> I would like to have boy friends like other girls and go out on Saturday nites, but no boy will take me because I was born without a nose — although I am a good dancer and have a nice shape and my father buys me pretty clothes.
>
> *(Miss Lonelyhearts)*

A girl without a nose is monstrous, truly, yet it is hard not to laugh, particularly when she expresses her need for beauty and romance. A nice shape does not compensate for a noseless face. Perhaps it should, but it does not. Perhaps we should not laugh, either, but we do. Perhaps words should not take precedence over persons, but here (pretending for the moment the girl is real) they do. On the other hand, West does not permit us to indulge in cant. The letter's words spell out a troublesome truth, that this girl, however unfortunate, has tacky values. She would give a great deal to be Homecoming Queen. Victims can be insufferably vain, no less than Presidents, and pity can be primarily self-gratifying. My point is that in the first passage West is keeping certain suppositions intact — the value, for instance, of pity — while in the second he orders his words so that we have to recognize ourselves as we truly are, not as we might prefer to suppose we are. It is recognizing this difference that makes us laugh, and our laughter implies a major admission: that the idealist's absolute may finally be more significant, more real, than we mere mortals are.

We regard West loosely as a writer ahead of his time. I would say that it is specifically *Miss Lonelyhearts* that warrants this reputation, and that it anticipates in particular the work of Barth, Barthelme, Coover, Elkin, Gardner, Pynchon, of all those writers loosely bunched as comic whose humor, by trying its own limits, examines how language does and undoes us, what it gives and what it takes, what it may mean and what it may not, and if we are at last full of fear and wonder, we should be: Being is finally awful, no matter how we look at it.

Nathanael West
and the Persistence of Hope

Martin Tropp

One section of Nathanael West's first novel, *The Dream Life of Balso Snell,* contrasts sharply with the collegiate cleverness and schoolboy scatology of the entire work. Balso finds a diary in a hollow tree. Ostensibly the creation of a twelve-year-old schoolboy, John Gilson, the diary contains a case history of a pathological murder with sexual overtones. Gilson's Dostoyevskian persona, Raskolnikov, shares his namesake's obsession with the dimensions of his inner self. West's Raskolnikov writes,

> I can know nothing; I can have nothing; I must devote my whole life to the pursuit of a shadow. It is as if I were attempting to trace with the point of a pencil the shadow of the tracing pencil. I am enchanted with the shadow's shape and want very much to outline it; but the shadow is attached to the pencil and moves with it, never allowing me to trace its tempting form. Because of some great need, I am continually forced to make the attempt.

The most obvious side to this image is the negative one—the vainly striving pencil, the constantly elusive, ephemeral shadow, the futility of the whole endeavor. Yet West implies something else. Due to some "great need" the writer never ceases trying. He is "enchanted with the shadow's shape," seeking some answer, while the shadow itself, the answer, is linked in some way to the pencil, the instrument of striving. This image is behind much of West's later work. But readers have often seen only its negative side. In *Miss Lonelyhearts* especially, and to a lesser extent in *The Day of the Locust* and *A Cool Million,* there exist half-hidden indications of the potential, at least, for an answer to the endless search of West's characters for a way out of

From *Renascence* 31, no. 4 (Summer 1979). © 1979 by Marquette University.

their nightmare labyrinth. To follow this thread, it is necessary to distinguish two separate, related searches in the novels, reflecting two aspects of human nature and two categories of Westian seeker.

The statement of Raskolnikov about the pencil and shadow is, obviously, both literary and psychological. He writes immediately preceding this: "what is that thing in your brain? Indulge my commands and some day the great doors of your mind will swing open and allow you to enter and handle to your complete satisfaction the vague shapes and figures hidden there." We see here the goal of one Westian seeker—a goal and search extensively treated by critics of West. On a psychological quest, the Westian hero, a newspaperman or screenwriter, attempts to find the words to open the cave of his own subconscious in order to discover the motivation behind the actions which constitute his own case history. All Miss Lonelyhearts can find is a rock, while Tod Hackett sees himself, in his own painting of "The Burning of Los Angeles," picking up a "small stone to throw before continuing his flight." For Raskolnikov, as well as for the protagonists of *Miss Lonelyhearts* and *The Day of the Locust*, motivation finally remains shadow; it is the nature of the search which becomes significant. As critics have pointed out, these Westian heroes explore the abstract mind through the abstracts of words and psychological, intellectual concepts—using pencil and brush to trace shadows with shadows. One of the bodiless voices in Delehanty's, speaking of Miss Lonelyhearts, describes this dead end succinctly: "The trouble with him, the trouble with all of us, is that we have no outer life, only an inner one, and that by necessity."

In *Miss Lonelyhearts*, this is the situation faced by the nameless hero, by Shrike and by Mrs. Shrike. Forced by their own Raskolnikov-like awareness to trace the shadow, they cannot escape the interior maze into which they have stepped. Miss Lonelyhearts, the "modern priest," must constantly take confession and find absolution for his own soul. In his interior struggle, he becomes homosexual, saint, and god, trying to find the key to unlock his own psychological allegory. His failure, so extensively treated by critics of West, is at times generalized into a vision of the total failure of society. Yet this defeat is, on one level at least, similar to Raskolnikov's in its isolated, personal nature. In *Balso Snell*, John Gilson-Iago-Raskolnikov ends his diary with a revealing account of the events that grew out of his crime:

> Inside of my head the murder has become like a piece of sand inside the shell of an oyster. My mind has commenced to form a pearl around it. The idiot, the singer, his laugh, the knife, the river, my change of sex, all cover the murder just as the secretions of an oyster cover an irritating grain of sand. As the ac-

cumulations grow and become solidified, the original irritation disappears. If the murder continues to grow in size it may become too large for me to contain; then I am afraid it will kill me, just as the pearl eventually kills the oyster.

In the same way, Miss Lonelyhearts becomes lost in his search, until the pearl (the smooth, sea-worn rock) that grows within him kills him. In the final scene of the novel, he hears again the cry of help from the letter writers, a cry that has never deserted him — but it is buried far beneath the secretions of his own psyche. The "original irritation" has been lost, long in the past.

All of this had been predicted early in the novel by the mysterious disembodied voices Miss Lonelyhearts hears in Delehanty's bar and dismisses. They comment upon the nature of his psychological search: "He's an escapist. He wants to cultivate his interior garden. But you can't escape, and where is he going to find a market for the fruits of his personality?" They also prophesy the end of Miss Lonelyhearts's search and its futility: "Even if he were to have a genuine religious experience, it would be personal and so meaningless, except to a psychologist." They see that this "self-cultivation" is actually a dead end, leading only to a deeper involvement with the self, creating more barriers between Miss Lonelyhearts and the suffering humanity he hears crying out to him. Miss Lonelyhearts becomes, finally, alone with his pearl — a monk tending his interior garden.

The prophetic voices say more. They become, in fact, a key to understanding the two-sided nature of the image of pencil and shadow. Two of the voices present a choice:

> Well, that's the trouble with his approach to God. It's too damn literary — plain song. Latin poetry, medieval painting, Huysmans, stained-glass windows and crap like that.
> What I say is, after all one has to earn a living. We can't all believe in Christ, and what does the farmer care about art? He takes his shoes off to get the warm feel of the rich earth between his toes. You can't take your shoes off in church.

The medieval and religious trappings the voices use to categorize Miss Lonelyhearts's approach to God suggest how out of touch he is with the people who ask him for help. His path to Christ becomes the "Christ complex," a dead end of psychological self-analysis, a meaningless and personal failure.

After Miss Lonelyhearts hears these voices he remembers Sundays in his childhood when he played the piano as his sister danced. His mind moves outward; he glimpses the patterns that have eluded him: "As Miss Lonelyhearts stood at the bar, swaying slightly to the remembered music, he thought of children dancing. Square replacing oblong and being replaced by circle. Every child, everywhere; in the whole world there was not one child who was not gravely, sweetly dancing." The dance of life, the universal harmony and beauty Miss Lonelyhearts glimpses is only a passing vision. Miss Lonelyhearts's swaying turns into "anger swung in large drunken circles" as he rejects the choice presented to him: "What in Christ's name was this Christ business? And children gravely dancing? He would ask Shrike to be transferred to the sports department." Immediately after this encounter, he returns to his interior maze and adds another layer to his pearl, as he goes out with Gates to torment an old man while playing psychologist. He had looked, briefly, at the possibilities the voices offer (" 'Was their nonsense the only barrier?' he asked himself. 'Had he been thwarted by such a low hurdle?' " and later finds a moment of happiness on a farm with Betty. But he, like Shrike, is lost in words. He can find no place in the dance. Yet, in a sense, it is all around him.

Most of the book is, of course, an expression of the futility of finding an answer to the violent suffering of humanity. This emptiness has been seen as the essence of West's landscape, a wasteland with "no hope of salvation." But what of those children "gravely, sweetly dancing"? In the letters, we see again this almost forgotten dance. It seems still to go on, holding out the hope of something solid and beautiful in the chaos of the novel's universe.

The obvious thing one notices about the letters — and the only thing that Miss Lonelyhearts notices — is that they contain tales of horrible suffering. The writers are in the crowd of people with "broken hands and torn mouths" which torments his mind. Yet it is also important to note that the writers see their suffering as outside of their own minds, based upon some physical defect or environmental condition. "Sick-of-it-all" complains of the pain in her kidneys; "Harold S." writes of the abuse of his deaf and dumb sister: "Desperate" describes the terrible consequences of a congenital deformity. The anguished cry of "Broad Shoulders," though less obviously based upon physiological factors than the others, and, partly because of that the most horrible, still consists of her reaction to the clear external factor of a sadistic husband. Contrast these letters with the letter Shrike composes from Miss Lonelyhearts to Christ:

Dear Miss Lonelyhearts of Miss Lonelyhearts —

I am twenty-six years old and in the newspaper game. Life for me is a desert empty of comfort. I cannot find pleasure in food, drink, or women — nor do the arts give me joy any longer. . . . All is desolation and a vexation of the spirit. I feel like hell. . . .

These self-indulgent complaints, even taking Shrike's satirical purpose into account, stand in sharp contrast to the tangible, physical scars of the letter writers. They experience pain born of life, not abstracted from it. Their scars are visible, as are their tormentors. They feel the irritation, and not the pearl.

Of course, one may say that the psychological torment undergone by Miss Lonelyhearts is more horrible precisely because there are no physical scars to which he can point. For the letter writers as well, the correction of the external emblems of their suffering — the missing nose, the deformed leg, the vicious husband — may not relieve their anguish. But the suffering Miss Lonelyhearts sees in them is not the suffering they feel. They believe that their pain can be erased with its visible signs, and thus they see something tangible to fight, and can ask Miss Lonelyhearts for an equally tangible solution.

The strength of the letter writers is that they fight the war in life that Miss Lonelyhearts battles in the dead-end cave of his mind. His only final tangible desire is for more words with which to answer the letter writers, while the writers themselves seek concrete solutions. They don't want the religious or philosophical platitudes Miss Lonelyhearts dishes out. Instead they seek clear answers to what are, to them, clear problems. They want to find out, in Sick-of-it-all's words, "what to do," whether it is as final as Desperate's "Ought I commit suicide?" or as practical as Harold S.'s "So please what would you do if the same hapened [sic] in your family," or as specific as Broad Shoulders's "Shall I take my husband back? How can I support my children?"

In "Some Notes on *Miss Lonelyhearts*," West declares "Psychology has nothing to do with reality nor should it be used as motivation." Reality motivates the letter writers; it is from the outside world that their problems come, and it is to an outside source that they apply for solutions. They are part of the "dance of life" — a grotesque ballet to be sure, but one which is, at least, vital. It is this dance that the writers want to order, and it is their belief that they can find a better place that keeps the dance alive. The pencil of their striving is, then, real, moved by faith; the changing shadow dances before them. The result is a simpler, purer formulation of the goal of Miss Lonelyhearts's futile search.

In Broad Shoulders's letter especially, one can see how the fusion of style and content brings forth the essence of what is tragic, noble, and strangely beautiful in the acceptance and participation of the flow of life. The longest letter in West's novel, it occupies a central, special place. Miss Lonelyhearts reads it when he returns from the country; it propels him further into his interior garden. Yet he reads it for his own purposes, "for the same reason that an animal tears at a wounded foot: to hurt the pain." He never listens to the voice in the letter, which tells a tale of almost unbelievable suffering while maintaining a delicate structure of control and dignity. The syntax, sentence length, and spelling begin to fall apart as she comes closer to the central incident—the day her husband hides under the bed in order to terrify her. Short clauses, strung together with simple connectives, catch us up in the onrushing flow of events. The horror emerges from a series of real, tangible indignities which pile up as, in a jumble of words, the writer breathlessly pours out her life. Yet, rising out of these horrors is not the cry of a wounded animal, or even a reaction of hatred and utter despair. Though sickened and brutalized, Broad Shoulders, as her name implies, manages to bear her burdens and keep hold of her dignity.

The impression that one gets from the body of the letter is, obviously, that the writer is not educated. She is not like Miss Lonelyhearts; words do not come easily. This is evident from the punctuation and the consistent misspellings which cannot be blamed upon emotional stress. She uses vulgar clichés, such as "fighting for Uncle Sam" and "$15 dollars per." But she also attempts, especially at the beginning and end of the letter, when we feel she is most in control of herself, to use the conventions of formal letter writing ("Thanking you for anything you can advise me in I remain yours truly"). She tries to use "cultivated" expressions ("unbeknown to me") and metaphors ("but debts collected . . . it almost took a derick to lift them"). The most jarring example of this incongruity of style and content occurs when she uses the euphemisms of polite society. Though she suffers like an animal, she still writes, "a baby boy was added to our union," and "I was put in financial embarasment." Her tone of deference emphasizes the great gulf between Miss Lonelyhearts and his supplicants, while the fact that she often uses these terms improperly, or misspells them, adds to the pathetic, yet courageous quality of the letter, and enhances the meaning of her final question, "Every woman is intitiled to a home isnt she?" Despite all that she has gone through, Broad Shoulders has not descended to the level of her tormentors; she still hopes for a better future. It is these moments, which occur in all the letters, that stand out, making the writers rise above the violence-ridden mob. They are all gentle people, "grave and sweet" but also simple and patient. They have faith, and dreams; although forced at times to cry for help, they would all like simply to ask for justice.

What, then, is West intending through the contrast of these two approaches to life—the inner and outer search, the interior garden and the dance of life? Keeping in mind the overall hopelessness which permeates and indeed smothers everyone and everything in the novel, one still gets a distinct impression of two diverging approaches to the problem of human suffering. The fruitless strivings of the wordsmiths such as Shrike and Miss Lonelyhearts are best clarified by turning to Dostoyevski, John Gilson-Raskolnikov's model, and particularly to *Notes from Underground:*

> I beg you, gentlemen, to listen sometimes to the moans of an educated man . . . a man who is "divorced from the soil and the national principles" as they call it these days. His moans become nasty, disgustingly spiteful, and go on for whole days and nights. And after all, he himself knows that he does not benefit at all from his moans; he knows better than anyone that he is only lacerating and irritating himself and others in vain; he knows that even the audience for whom he is exerting himself and his whole family now listen to him with loathing, do not believe him for a minute, and that deep down they understand that he could moan differently, more simply, without trills and flourishes, and that he is only indulging himself like that out of spite, out of malice.

Miss Lonelyhearts, cultivating his interior garden, growing his own pearl, with a vast distance between himself and the objects of his pity, never sees the alternative of "moan[ing] differently." He reads the letters and reads his suffering into them, using their words for his own private scourge.

West never clearly presents the letter writers' response to suffering as an alternative for Miss Lonelyhearts, or indeed for the reader. He simply suggests two ways of living, and the great gulf separating them. In *A Cool Million* West points up the absurdity of optimism in the face of physical suffering, as Lemuel Pitkin retains his boyish pluck and cheery good nature while he is systematically dismantled by a heartless society. Even here, though, there is a suggestion that Lem's reserve of trust and hope is a national resource that has been strip mined and desecrated, but never exhausted. Finally, in his last novel, *The Day of the Locust,* West comes closest to defining the way of the letter writers, and its resulting beauty, order, and value.

At Harry Greener's funeral, Tod Hackett hears a Bach chorale, "Come Redeemer, Our Saviour":

> Tod recognized the music. His mother often played a piano adaptation of it on Sundays at home. It very politely asked Christ to come, in clear and honest tones with just the proper amount of supplication. The God it invited was not the King of Kings, but a shy and gentle Christ, a maiden surrounded by maidens, and the invitation was to a lawn fete, not to the home of some weary, suffering sinner. It didn't plead; it urged with infinite grace and delicacy, almost as though it were afraid of frightening the prospective guest.

"Now come, O our Saviour," the music begged. Gone was its diffidence and no longer was it polite. Its struggle with the bass had changed it. Even a hint of a threat crept in and a little impatience. Of doubt, however, he could not detect the slightest trace. . . . "Come or don't come," the music seemed to say, "I love you and my love is enough." It was a simple statement of fact, neither cry nor serenade, made without arrogance or humility.

Like the piano music Miss Lonelyhearts played for his sister while "waiting . . . for their father to come home from church," this piece reminds Tod Hackett of childhood Sundays and gives him a glimpse of the depth of faith underlying a world of suffering—the dance that is the rhythm of life and its hope of redemption. But, like Miss Lonelyhearts and friends, Tod Hackett and his companions can now respond only to themselves: "So far as Tod could tell, no one was listening to the music. Faye was sobbing and the others seemed busy inside themselves. Bach politely serenading Christ was not for them." The music is soon silenced in mid-phrase, and Tod rushes out of the funeral parlor.

The beauty of this attitude, the music of the letter writers, is extended in *The Day of the Locust* to the lyric song of birds. Though all the main characters in the novel are corrupted, and the "dance of life" is parodied in a brutal cockfight, the moments that hold out the possibility of "moaning differently" come when, as at the funeral, West describes a lyrical song arising from the cacophony of suffering. Thus, when Tod and Earle go hunting, they hear the song of the quail, "full of melancholy and weariness, yet marvelously sweet. Still another quail joined the duet. This one called from near the center of the field. It was a trapped bird, but the sound it made had no anxiety in it, only sadness, impersonal and without hope." Even though the trapped bird is without hope and about to die, it can still join in the song; an indefinable beauty and dignity arises from the fact that such a duet can nevertheless be sung.

But the song of birds gives Tod a brief moment of hope. After the quail are eaten, Tod and Earle watch Faye and Miguel do their mating dance. Earle knocks Miguel unconscious, then Tod pursues the fleeing Faye. He falls and lies quietly with his face "in a clump of wild mustard that smelled of the rain and sun, clean, fresh and sharp," listening to the "low rich music" of a bird:

The bird began to sing again. When it stopped. Faye was forgotten and he only wondered if he weren't exaggerating the importance of the people who come to California to die. Maybe they weren't really desperate enough to set a single city on fire, let alone the whole country. Maybe they were only the pick of America's madmen and not at all typical of the rest of the land.

Of course, he soon changes "pick of America's madmen" to "cream," convinced that "the milk from which it had been skimmed was just as rich in violence. . . . There would be civil war." By the time he stands up to look for Faye, the message of the bird's song is forgotten.

This reading of West's two major novels leaves us with Miss Lonelyhearts, Tod Hackett, and those like them, cut off from the "dance of life," only dimly aware of its music, and the memories it stirs, but rejecting them for the self-destructive creation of pearls of private suffering. Their search is desolate and shadowy, through the mind's recesses, their only responses indulgent, irritating, and totally futile. From this search we feel the most despair. West, however, shows us another answer. Though the letter writers' tragic song seems equally fruitless, and perhaps finally as absurd as Lemuel Pitkin's unbending faith, one still feels a beauty and dignity ennobling their endeavors. Finally, it is this quiet unsolicited faith and beauty, expressed by West in *Miss Lonelyhearts* through the dance and the letters and in *The Day of the Locust* through the chorale and the song of the birds, that comes closest to giving us reason to hope. We are reminded of the last stanzas of Thomas Hardy's poem "The Darkling Thrush":

> At once a voice arose among
>> The bleak twigs overhead
> In a full-hearted evensong
>> Of joy illimited;
> An aged thrush, frail, gaunt, and small,
>> In blast-beruffled plume,
> Had chosen thus to fling his soul
>> Upon the growing gloom.
>
> So little cause for carolings
>> Of such ecstatic sound
> Was written on terrestrial things
>> Afar or nigh around,
> That I could think there trembled through
>> His happy good-night air
> Some blessed Hope, whereof he knew
>> And I was unaware.

Nathanael West hints, at least, that there is a seemingly endless fund of belief and love in the world which, merely by existing, helps purify the wasteland of his novels.

Letters and Spirit
in *Miss Lonelyhearts*

Mark Conroy

The Scene of Typing

An advice-to-the-lovelorn columnist whose advice is often worse than no advice, and who knows it, has many reasons to want to escape into daydream. This pastor's son has as his most significant dream that of salvation through, and ultimately as, Jesus Christ. But before that consumes his life, there are smaller dreams, and although their goal is to take him out of an imprisonment, they often return him there more forcibly. In Nathanael West's novel, *Miss Lonelyhearts*, all the title character's dreams, all his forms of escape, have a way of doing that.

One of the strongest dreams occurs as Miss Lonelyhearts, in typical paralysis before the newsroom typewriter where he produces his columns, sits and thinks instead of a desert:

> A desert . . . not of sand, but of rust and body dirt, surrounded by a back-yard fence on which are posters describing the events of the day. . . . Inside the fence Desperate, Broken-hearted, Disillusioned-with-tubercular-husband and the rest were gravely forming the letters MISS LONELYHEARTS out of white-washed clam shells, as if decorating the lawn of a rural depot.

"Desperate," "Broken-hearted" and the rest are of course the letter writers that send queries to his columns; but their names are monikers created by and for the newspaper, and the fence that rings them in with the day's events is the newspaper itself: that which imprisons both the columnist and the readers, and binds them to one another. They exist for him only through

From *The University of Windsor Review* 17, no. 1 (Fall/Winter 1982). © 1982 by the University of Windsor Review.

their letters, he for them only in his replies. Yet not content with the stories these characters invent for themselves, he invents his *own* for them. In his story, they spell out his name as an object of worship—which means, ironically, that they are as much Miss Lonelyhearts's creators as his dupes. In dreaming his readers' dreams of him, Miss Lonelyhearts realizes that their dreams allow "Miss Lonelyhearts" to exist as a name, and its bearer to pursue his trade.

Paradoxically, this scene recalls him to his task; after all, the readers' faith in his name requires Miss Lonelyhearts to help them form its letters by forming his own letters. His typing, however, is again interrupted:

> He could not go on with it and turned again to the imagined desert where Desperate, Broken-hearted and the others were still building his name. They had run out of sea shells and were using faded photographs, soiled fans, timetables, playing cards, broken toys, imitation jewellery—junk that memory had made precious, far more precious than anything the sea might yield.

The column, it appears, consists of the mutual effort of writer and reader to construct a saving name, not from nature but from the runic fragments of discourse and human fabrication: timetables, photographs, playing cards. The name they build must somehow yield the meaning of the junk of its decay.

The prospects for genuine redemption, as opposed to temporary balm, are not good, though, because Miss Lonelyhearts soon has another dream of detritus, and here it is *he* who does the forming, not his readers. His daydream features the cultural remnants similar to those of the earlier dreams. He finds himself "in the window of a pawnshop full of fur coats, diamond rings, watches . . . the paraphernalia of suffering." They are not such in themselves, certainly, but only by virtue of their situation in the pawnshop. Still, Miss Lonelyhearts, sensing a "tropism for disorder" among these objects, joins battle with chaos:

> First he formed a phallus of old watches and rubber boots, then a heart of umbrellas and trout flies. . . . But nothing proved definitive and he began to make a gigantic cross. When the cross became too large for the pawnshop, he moved it to the shore of the ocean.

This dream, parallel with the first, makes it clear that Miss Lonelyhearts is a Miss Lonelyhearts reader. Like the others, he uses the "paraphernalia of suffering" of a pawnshop to erect a variety of symbols by which the suffering can be redeemed: a project for forming legible meaning from the spoor of failure. He carries his readers' projects of redemptions back to the lifegiving sea, in an attempt to transcend the desert of the newspaper office; and his way of getting there begins with a sexual symbol and ends with a religious one—a development that will be seen to mime that of the book as a whole. Whether in practice he ever *actually* gets to the life-giving sea of renewal we explore below.

In addition to the fact that Miss Lonelyhearts's way of retrieving meaning from cultural debris is the same as his readers', the setting is also very similar, the pawnshop suggesting the newspaper office as did the fenced-in desert. This columnist's fantasy visions, whether of his readers' attempts to give meaning to their suffering or his own, can only exist within the prison of the newspaper office. He can be a saviour, they a faithful flock, only insofar as the paper allows both to exist linguistically, as words. Indeed, whenever Miss Lonelyhearts confronts his readers in the flesh, the results are disastrous.

The pawnshop image itself is a clue as to why this dream may well end in disaster. A pawnshop is a place where its customers' misfortunes are exploited for money, just as the Miss Lonelyhearts column has its origin as a cynical circulation gimmick, where his replies to his readers' problems are cruel jokes that function as further posters on the fence of the desert. Thus does every attempt to escape this doomed condition return Miss Lonelyhearts all the more forcibly to it.

THE WORLD ACCORDING TO SHRIKE: ORIGIN AS PARODY

The dreams may be Miss Lonelyhearts's invention, but his column is not. It is the brainchild of the newspaper's city editor, Willie Shrike, to whom Miss Lonelyhearts owes his name (and so his identity); and like his name, the words he writes are not his, though he writes them, owes his existence to them. His first reply in the novel, in fact, is dictated by Shrike:

> "*Art is a Way Out.*"
> "Do not let life overwhelm you. When the old paths are choked with the debris of failure, look for newer and fresher paths. Art is just such a path. Art is distilled from suffering . . ."
> "For those who have not the talent to create, there is appreciation . . . "

It is ironic that Shrike emphasizes Miss Lonelyhearts's bondage by dictating a letter that speaks of a spurious "way out" through suffering; doubly ironic that he dictates a recommendation of the saving, creative power of art. It is a complete perversion of the "personal expression" in language that not only Miss Lonelyhearts but also his colleagues and his boss once believed in:

> At college, and perhaps for a year afterwards, they had believed in literature, had believed in Beauty and in personal expression as an absolute end. When they lost this belief, they lost everything. Money and fame meant nothing to them. They were not world-ly men.

At the newspaper they are as far removed from personal expression as possible; the relentless mechanism of the paper and its cynical relation to its audience are personified by Shrike, and the other newspapermen are the objects of his sinister ventriloquism: "Like Shrike, the man they imitated, they were machines for making jokes. A button machine makes buttons, no matter what the power used, foot, steam or electricity. They, no matter what the motivating force, death, love or God, made jokes." They all imitate Shrike as machines would, but Shrike himself is a kind of mechanism: all are caught in the infernal machine of the paper.

Miss Lonelyhearts's project is to forge from this empty language the possibility of genuine redemption: if the cynical fictions he is required to write are actively taken over by the writer, then perhaps they will be rendered true. The relentless machine of the typewriter must be sublated, and the Promethean pen must replace subservience before the typewriter (where an earlier draft of this novel has a bemused Miss Lonelyhearts mention he composed his first love letters!). If the joke can, by a change of intention, cease to be a joke, then the writer's pledges can be redeemed along with the suffering of his readers, in the same way that the paraphernalia of suffering in a pawnshop can be redeemed.

That this change of heart might not succeed in reversing the columnist's role from victim to saviour is clear from another dream, related to those above, where Miss Lonelyhearts is a magician who makes doorknobs flower and speak at his command. But when it comes time to "lead his audience in prayer," ventriloquism once again intervenes: "But no matter how hard he struggled, his prayer was one Shrike had taught him and his voice was that of a conductor calling stations." Not only Miss Lonelyhearts's language but also the circumstances in which he enunciates it are determined by Shrike (or rather, by the same cynical exigencies that determine Shrike's behaviour). However sincere, his prayers come out as Shrike has dictated them.

Shrike constantly refers to the need for the circulation to multiply; Goldsmith, one of Shrike's imitators, tells Miss Lonelyhearts to respond to a sexually frustrated letter writer by determining to "get the lady with child and increase the potential circulation of the paper." The reproduction of life is to serve the newspaper rather than vice versa. And indeed the general pattern in this text is that the manic productivity of civilization has produced no spiritual regeneration. The protagonist sees the explosion of productivity that produced the city as destructive frenzy: "an orgy of stonebreaking," he calls it. And the existing civilization is the stone that "would someday break them [i.e., the Americans]." Many of Miss Lonelyhearts's readers have also been financially and psychologically broken by the repetitive activity of the economic system; one thinks of Doyle the cripple, and also, inevitably, of the text's 1932 publication date.

Miss Lonelyhearts, then, is broken like the readers of his columns, but over his typewriter, not the wheel. The same mechanism that can reproduce language to infinity without sympathy or even comprehension adheres to Shrike's own discourse, machinelike letter without spirit. Shrike's name is already, of course, a parodic anagram for "Christ," but he is not sufficiently demonic to be an anti-christ: he is at best, as one of the chapters calls him, a dead Pan. The nickname works on two levels, since in Shrike one finds the incarnation of the boundless capacity for parody and joke-telling founded on the failure of Eros. If his practical jokes seem to have an air of the sadistic, this should not be surprising; they are used as compensation for the lack of true sexual power, in a pattern that Miss Lonelyhearts also imitates (at least at first). Shrike's relation to his wife bears out this sadistic hint: unable to please her himself, he still maintains dominion over her, in a parody of the male role. As Mary Shrike tells Miss Lonelyhearts:

> "Do you know why he lets me go out with other men? To save money. He knows that I let them neck me and when I get home all hot and bothered, why he climbs into my bed and begs for it. The cheap bastard!"

Shrike's lovemaking at best pleases himself at the expense of frustrating both his wife and her other men; and it is a question whether it even pleases Shrike. ("Sleeping with her is like sleeping with a knife in one's groin," he tells Miss Lonelyhearts.) Shrike's victimization and his glib rhetoric are of a piece, and his sadistic ironies shield his own impotence.

In taking out Shrike's wife, Miss Lonelyhearts indulges in a bit of sadism himself; one suspects the real quarry here is Shrike rather than Mary. But the columnist becomes a part of the scheme whereby Shrike, in his own inadequacy, victimizes others in turn. As Miss Lonelyhearts attempts to "drag Mrs. Shrike to the floor," she demands to be released: "Then he heard footsteps . . . the door opened and Shrike looked into the corridor. He had on only the top of his pajamas." It seems that even in his off hours, Miss Lonelyhearts still works for Shrike, is still his victim.

This sadism has as its condition the unredemptive, unregenerative sexual-

that is imaged in the text by various distortions of nature: ". . . there were no signs of spring. The decay that covered the surface of the mottled ground was not the kind in which life generates." The Eliotic wasteland imagery has been remarked by other critics, and the title character in this text bears some resemblance to Eliot's Fisher King. One could even say that Shrike is a walking wasteland of cultural detritus, though that fact indicates some of the difference between West's world and Eliot's. Whereas in Eliot the reclamation of the Indo-European cultural heritage would revivify the wasteland with the "peace which passeth understanding," West by contrast presents a universe where that attempt has already fallen under the ban of Shrike's sterile parody. Though the iconography remains, it cannot inspire the belief of other times. The fragments Miss Lonelyhearts has shored against his ruin are themselves already ruins.

The fact that the culture is decaying would explain the decay Miss Lonelyhearts finds in his urban park near the office: the little park that he says needs a drink. For all his girlfriend Betty's conviction that his problems are city problems, their weekend in Connecticut confronts images that partake of the city park: "Although spring was well advanced, in the deep shade there was nothing but death—rotten leaves, gray and white fungi, and over everything a funereal hush."

To bring renewal to this decay, Miss Lonelyhearts wishes his readers would "water the soil with their tears. Flowers would then spring up, flowers that smelled of feet." This comic image is an ironical use of what, like the sea, are potent symbols of regeneration. The agent of this flowering is his readers' tears, suffering its own means of redemption. Indeed, the park vision in its essence is feminine: not only because of the Mary Magdalene image of tears and feet, but also because it is initiated by the "shadow of a lamp-post" that pierces him "like a spear." But this confusion is a part of his dilemma: how to make passive suffering the agent of overcoming. The appeal of Christ as a model for this *via negativa* is obvious, and upon returning from Connecticut Miss Lonelyhearts endeavours to propose the Christ vision explicitly, but cannot: "He snatched the paper out of the machine. With him, even the word Christ was a vanity."

Christ's name is early on identified with the redemptive power of language: ". . . something stirred in him when he shouted the name of Christ, something secret and enormously powerful." He also figures the triumph of the soul through suffering, of course; and Miss Lonelyhearts hopes that his linguistic bondage to the repetitive dead language of the paper will yield redemptive discourse not only because his own suffering makes him similar to his readers, but also because remorse over his own complicity in their exploitation will bring the necessary humility to accept the mystical solution. If those two reasons sound contradictory, they are; but both spring equally from a situation of writing that breeds suffering equal to that of his correspondents. Still, it is his complicity in the initial exploitation that keeps Miss Lonelyhearts from really fusing with his readers; true, he suffers as his readers do, but for him suffering is indissociable from guilt. The readers are unknowing victims, but the columnist is knowing: a party to his own exploitation, and to the same extent, that of his readers. His female name expresses the predicament: he is the perpetrator of a hoax, but also a passive sufferer under it.

The price then, of bondage to Shrike is an emasculated language which increasingly takes over Miss Lonelyhearts's life. The fraudulent discourse becomes its own curse after a while. (As mentioned earlier, his colleagues are also riddled with self-contempt. The revealing exchange where various newspapermen at the speakeasy fantasize "gang bangs" of famous women novelists is fitting, since for a woman to attain something of their own forsaken ideal of personal expression must be further unwanted proof of their linguistic emasculation!) The glib rhetoric and endless punning of Shrike signify the same impotence as that displayed by the readers with their "inarticulate and impotent," and ungrammatical, letters. His abdication of any true self-expression is the precondition for Shrike's sterile patter. In a way, the empty articulateness of Shrike or Miss Lonelyhearts is more severe a condition than the words of the letter writers, or the balletic hands of Doyle as they shadow forth his suffering. At the least, they give some voice to grief. Shrike, by contrast, manages this only once, in evoking the true hell of life with Mary. But both glibness and inarticulateness contain formidable latent aggressions, as becomes clear below.

Miss Lonelyhearts is different from Shrike in that he wishes to break through glibness and cliché to some ideal of authentic speech. When he attempts such speech, though, his tongue becomes a "fat thumb." Like his readers, he loses the ability to articulate his thoughts at precisely the moment when they are most important to him: as he is explaining to Betty his position on the newspaper and his attitude toward it. He begins to "shout at her, accompanying his shouts with gestures [that resemble] those of an old-fashioned actor." This scene is repeated later when he is at home with Betty, and Betty advises him to stop "making a fool of yourself" by avoiding his job. He replies with his own Miss Lonelyhearts story, told in the third person, recapitulating his absurd vocation to the point where he "discovers that his correspondents take him seriously. For the first time in his life, he is forced to examine the values by which he lives. This examination shows him that he is the victim of the joke and not its perpetrator." Though more articulate than his first attempt, it is still blunted on Betty ("he saw that Betty still thought him a fool").

Like his dreams, the story he tells Betty is an approach to his predicament. He is not usually in the position of asking for advice or expressing suffering, as he here does; more typically he *gives* advice or alleviates suffering (in theory). The column begins as exploitation disguised as service; but his encounter with his victims as individuals gives his own culpability some clarity. This is why his formulation that he is victim and not perpetrator could be amended; he is both victim *and* perpetrator, indeed victim *insofar* as perpetrator.

Ironically, this figure is seen by Shrike as a priest of twentieth-century America; his characteristic posture is that of hearing confession. In a society where failure is sin, advice for its banishment is absolution. But if Miss Lonelyhearts could genuinely absolve his readers with healing speech, his own pain would be removed along with theirs. The trouble is that the remedy has been poisoned before the fact by its origin as parody. Much as he mocks Betty's belief that all evil is sickness to be cured ("No morality, only medicine"), her medicinal approach is not far from his own naivete in assuming that words infused with the proper spirit can heal.

When Miss Lonelyhearts tries to transmit his own belief in the efficacy of suffering for redemption, he becomes inarticulate like his readers, but in his case it takes the form of the slick rhetoric of the column. His readers' tongue-tied sincerity wars against the cynical patter of Shrike, producing a strange combination. He sees it at one point as owing to his avoidance of Christ: " . . . he had failed to tap the force in his heart and had merely written a column for his paper." Yet when he tries to bring up Christ at the Doyles' the results are even worse: "This time he had failed still more miserably. He had substituted the rhetoric of Shrike for that of Miss Lonelyhearts." The figure of Shrike and the column provide the measure of his failure to give genuine healing through speech. It is not that his hysterical speeches to the Doyles are not sincere, just that their form has already been inscribed by the pen (or typewriter) of Shrike's paper. When the columnist attempts to play his savior-role straight, the conventions within which he must do it—determined by the newspaper's management and ratified, despite the falsity of those conventions, by the readers—betray the pathos of that role. When he tries to legitimate his false role toward his audience, it becomes only more false. This is the paradox concealed in the fact that it is only when he understands that he is being *taken seriously* by his letter writers that he realizes he is also the victim of the joke he has helped to perpetrate.

STAGES ON MISS LONELYHEARTS'S WAY

Given this understanding of his own position as a writer addressing an audience under false pretenses, is there a pattern to Miss Lonelyhearts's attempts to work through the predicament that haunts his dreams, daydreams and language?

The fitful alternation between frantic activity and catatonic passivity in the character of Miss Lonelyhearts has been noted by others. Some have traced this trait to that psychology associated with hysteria, that "snake whose scales are tiny mirrors in which the dead world takes on a semblance of life." The violent imagery of West seems to support this view. One of the commentators on *Miss Lonelyhearts,* Randall Reid, has pointed out that the febrile imagery is not only indicative of the protagonist's hysterical state, but also of a genuine state of affairs; so what Reid calls hysteria, and what we might call passive-aggressive behaviour, reflects Miss Lonelyhearts's imprisonment in a situation that requires him to parody a redeemer's role. We argue that it is his status as a *writer* that compels his behaviour: behaviour which oscillates between passive withdrawal and active delusion in an attempt to transcend an enforced false relationship with his readership. Roughly speaking, there are five stages that lead up to the protagonist's final ironic apotheosis:

1. Anger at his impotence in the face of Shrike and his paper, with two results: the attempt to use his position to sexual advantage, and sadism directed against various targets. (The two are related, since sex, as we have seen, is generally used here in an aggressive way.) He tries unsuccessfully to seduce Shrike's wife in an indirect foray against the editor, but this sally only confirms his bondage to and victimization by Shrike. The second, more fateful, attempt involves a letter writer, Fay Doyle.

With Fay's letter, a complaint about being married to a cripple, the prospect of spiritual nourishment looms again in adulterous sex. This time he is successful, though Fay is as much the seducer as seduced: "He had always been the pursuer, but now found a strange pleasure in having the roles reversed." Mrs. Doyle is a sea image, of course (Miss Lonelyhearts crawls out of bed "like an exhausted swimmer leaving the surf"). Thus, when he cannot advance his own aggressive interests on those who have rhetorical and institutional power over him, he practices his designs on a reader, over whom *he* has some power. But even this sadistic move is only partly successful, ending with a lengthy tale of woe related by Fay, to which, as usual, Miss Lonelyhearts must listen sympathetically. The climatic incident in the speakeasy with the Clean Old Man brings these sadistic impulses to a head, as Miss Lonelyhearts viciously twists the old man's arm to torture him into telling the "story of your life." The frustration and sadism of the columnist's role are clearest at this point, and the scene will be echoed later in the text.

2. Attempt to escape the columns and the attendant sense of futility: what could be called the "suburban solution." He retreats first to his room (in the chapter "Miss Lonelyhearts in the Dismal Swamp"), then to Connecticut with Betty. Of course, Shrike, who bursts into Miss Lonelyhearts's sickroom before he leaves, has already satirized this possibility of escape (along with the escapes of hedonism, the South Seas, suicide, art, and drugs) in a series of bombastic set pieces.

Despite Shrike's malediction, Miss Lonelyhearts and Betty go to Connecticut for a pseudo-pastoral interval. It is not only nature but nature's story that is competing with his gloom, as Betty's stories of her childhood on a farm are proffered as an antidote to his own story. This itself gives a clue to the failure of nature as an escape: Betty has already made a cliché of nature, one which has been parodied by Shrike. Nature as an imagined scene of plenitude is a figure of cultural fantasy, and so his union with nature and its story, figured in his sexual union with Betty—now "wholesome" rather than "sick" sex—is still not proof against the Bronx slums through which they return from Connecticut's impossible suburban space.

3. Decision to use the new fully conscious sense of his own degradation to effect his readers' salvation. He feels at this stage that he has not allowed the Christ dream to emerge "not so much because of Shrike's jokes or his own self-doubt, but because of his lack of humility." He begins cultivating this humility, and avoiding Betty as well. His visit to the Doyles is the culmination of his attempt to bring the message of suffering as redemption through Christ. It is initiated by accident and ends in disaster. Miss Lonelyhearts is trying to read the cripple Doyle's letter, which he has been handed, when their hands inadvertently touch:

> He jerked away, but then drove his hand back and forced it to clasp the cripple's. After finishing the letter, he did not let go, but pressed it firmly with all the love he could manage. At first the cripple covered his embarrassment by disguising the meaning of the clasp with a handshake, but he soon gave in to it and they sat silently hand in hand.

This kind of grotesquely painful social awkwardness is something that initiates the elaborate series of false steps and misinterpretations between Miss Lonelyhearts and Doyle that melodramatically recurs in the last chapter. Nor do the cross-purposes augur well for the session at the Doyles where, amid the couple's ill-concealed mutual hatred, Miss Lonelyhearts tries to "find a message" to give them. It is at this point that he realizes he has only written a column for the newspaper and imitated, against his intention, the rhetoric of Shrike.

4. A second retreat from the column, this one more severe. It is this sequence that is presided over by the image of the rock: a metaphor for passive withdrawal. When Shrike bursts into Miss Lonelyhearts's room during his hideout, as is Shrike's wont, Miss Lonelyhearts does not yield: "Shrike dashed against him, but fell back, as a wave that dashes against an ancient rock, smooth with experience, falls back."

The nature of Miss Lonelyhearts's withdrawal, his passivity, is worthy of note: a withdrawal from speech and specifically from the narratives of his column. The false reciprocity of his column has been a story of redemption in exchange for a story of woe, but by this point Miss Lonelyhearts has clearly abdicated his part of the exchange. In the chapter entitled "Miss Lonelyhearts Attends a Party," he utters not a recorded word. But then the party is just another ploy to humiliate him, in the form of a game called "Everyman his own Miss Lonelyhearts," which involves a batch of his (presumably as yet unanswered) letters from the cityroom. Says Shrike: " 'First, each of you will do his best to answer one of these letters, then, from your answers, Miss Lonelyhearts will diagnose your moral ills.' " It so happens that the letter he distributes to Miss Lonelyhearts is Doyle's death threat, prompted by his wife's contention—which ironically is untrue—that Miss Lonelyhearts tried to rape her. The letter is read by Shrike, because the letter's intended recipient has silently left the party without removing the letter from its envelope.

In rejecting the letters, in refusing to read the message and abdicating his Miss Lonelyhearts role, he does not "get the message" of his own peril. The letter is a prediction, the more because its addressee has not read it. Everyone in the book has a Miss Lonelyhearts story, including columnist and editor. Both the columnist's professional and his sexual lives have relied upon an exchange of stories: Mary Shrike has a tale of woe, Betty a tale of innocence, etc. In the wake of failure as a healer, he is now weary of the surfeit of narratives that endlessly repeat the stories of the tellers' lives without ultimate cure. So he withdraws—from the letters, from his professional position, and from his own past exploitation. This break with his past writing situation he sees as a way of detaching himself from Shrike's joke.

But his refusal to be the butt of Shrike's joke only insures that he will be the victim of a more earnest joke with a fatal punch-line. Miss Lonelyhearts has refused to read the story of his own life: of his past complicity in the deceptions that made his linguistic life possible, and of his future peril from an admirer who has discovered his fradulence and illegitimacy. (Fay's rape story is a lie, but its profounder truth is that Doyle has been cuckolded in a sexual betrayal that is also a linguistic one: Doyle could, after all, be any reader whose trust Miss Lonelyhearts has transgressed.) His renunciation of the letter in favour of the spirit of a Christ that he will not have to "handle . . . with a thick glove of words" seals his doom. His own past is inscribed in Doyle's letter and, because the message is not received, his atonement as well.

In the subsequent chapter, Miss Lonelyhearts's conversation with Betty only confirms his divorce from language. Although he does speak with her, he blandly fobs her off with things he feels she wants to hear: he tells her he is working for an ad agency, he begs her to marry him, for this reason. He feels guiltless about this because his withdrawal from language (that is, from any connection between language and truth) is complete: "He did not feel guilty. He did not feel. The rock was a solidification of his feeling. . . ." Ironically, this dialogue with Betty is a further negation of his own past ties to his earlier aggressive sexuality. In this sense, his position parallels that of Betty, who offers to abort their illegitimate child, and so remove a reminder of the common burden of their past.

5. Miss Lonelyhearts's momentary dyslexia now culminates in what West acidly calls a "religious experience." In another failed dialectical reversal, he rises, after lying abed for three days, on the third day and foresees a new career as Miss Lonelyhearts, only now twice-born. His call to grace takes the form of a repetition of his previous writing situation, with God taking Shrike's position:

> God said: "Will you accept it, now?"
> And he replied, "I accept, I accept."
> He immediately began to plan a new life and his future conduct as Miss Lonelyhearts. He submitted drafts of his column to God and God approved them. God approved his every thought.

Miss Lonelyhearts's letter to Christ—dictated by Shrike earlier in the text—has now been answered. The passive-aggressive oscillation now swung back to frenzied acceptance of the columnist-savior role, but on a mystical plane that will somehow transform shoddy advice into revelation: in the extreme of his delusion, Miss Lonelyhearts is indistinguishable from God. ("His heart was one heart, the heart of God. And his brain was likewise God's.") The aggressiveness of his mission is signaled by the "mentally unmotivated violence" that changes the rock into a furnace.

The promise is fulfilled by the arrival of the cripple Doyle, but lacking the message of Doyle's note, Miss Lonelyhearts radically misconstrues the meaning: "God had sent him so that Miss Lonelyhearts could perform a miracle and be certain of his conversion. It was a sign." A sign it surely is, but of rather a different sort. How different becomes clear when one sees that this ironic climax is the repetition of the climaxes of two previous chapters: chapters that suggest the dissonance between the true import of Doyle's actions and the victim's interpretation of it.

Doyle's act itself and its intent have been prefigured in the sordid close of the "Clean Old Man" incident. That scene directly depicts the frustrated sadism practiced by Miss Lonelyhearts at first against his editor, his fiancee and, of course, his readers. His seduction of Fay belongs to this early phase, though it occurs before he meets her husband. Doyle's revenge is thus the mirror of Miss Lonelyhearts's earlier impotent rage, and is also the fulfillment of a chain of events begun by Fay's seduction.

Miss Lonelyhearts sees his role as the opportunity, in the fullness of his divinity, to enact fully what he only awkwardly enacts in the scene where he and the cripple meet. He thinks: "He would embrace the cripple and the cripple would be made whole again, even as he, a spiritual cripple, had been made whole." As he was at the beginning, so now the born-again columnist is confronting his specular image in that of his readers; but he assumes that he has been healed, and so misreads the nature of his resemblance to Doyle. To be specific, this misconception allows him to ignore the "something wrapped in a newspaper" that Doyle is carrying, which is a pistol. His ignoral is symptomatic of his refusal to acknowledge the aggression lying within his *own* writing position, along with the equally aggressive consequences. (It is not surprising that, deluded as he is, Miss Lonelyhearts is incapable of "reading" what is really in the newspaper).

Trapped in the narrative of the Christ story, he does not recognize the story he is really in: the oldest story in the book, the adulterous triangle. He misunderstands Doyle's warning as a cry for help. His attempt to escape his past involvement with stories takes the form of another story, the Christ legend, which he persists in enacting and which only causes him to misread his own peril. His fate is a parody of the Christ story where resurrection on the third day is followed by crucifixion: the Christ story as Shrike no doubt would have written it. Miss Lonelyhearts is most completely the victim when he believes himself the saviour, and he is, of course, never more distant from his readers (whom Doyle represents) than when approaching his mystical union.

In *Miss Lonelyhearts*, the central narrative of Western culture produces no revivification, only the bloom of fever. It only makes possible the endless parodic repetitions of Shrike (who is conscious of the parody) and the manic delusions of Miss Lonelyhearts (who at the last is not). Miss Lonelyhearts's Christ dream betrays him as much as Shrike's Christ joke has betrayed his readers; he is in this respect as well, Doyle's *semblable.* Rather than allowing Miss Lonelyhearts to exchange his soulless typewriter for a Promethean pen producing lifegiving language, it leads him only to repeat Christ's role and his own subservient columnist's role, and the two roles fail to cohere. Like the many narratives Miss Lonelyhearts tries to escape, the Christ legend is doomed to the same fraudulence; as long as Miss Lonelyhearts is who he is, even the Christ dream is compromised fatally, like a compulsively recurring dream that ends only with the end of the dreamer.

The stories we tell ourselves, like the stories we tell others, are as necessary as they are fraudulent; and the more irrelevant they become, the more necessary they may well seem. The narrative of *Miss Lonelyhearts* is the story of this cruel calculus. It is a tale where Shrike has the last laugh, because he has already written the first line.

The Ritual Icon

Douglas Robinson

Miss Lonelyhearts is, at one level, an attempt to mediate allusively between two biblical texts, the apocalypse and the temptation of Christ in the wilderness; as such, it stands as a kind of American *Paradise Regained,* which also mediates between those two texts by internalizing the restoration of paradise, displacing the raising of Eden "in the waste wilderness" into the divine mind of Jesus Christ. The parallels between West's novel and Milton's brief epic are in fact striking enough to be taken seriously: whereas Milton has Satan describe Jesus as "Proof against all temptation as a rock/Of adamant, and as a center firm" (4:533–34), West tells us that "Miss Lonelyhearts stood quietly in the center of the room. Shrike dashed against him, but fell back, as a wave that dashes against an ancient rock, smooth with experience, falls back. There was no second wave." As in *Paradise Regained*, this rocklike immovability is Miss Lonelyhearts's only successful defense against a satanic Shrike: " 'Don't be a spoilsport,' Shrike said with a great deal of irritation. He was a gull trying to lay an egg in the smooth flank of a rock, a screaming, clumsy gull." Milton's Satan is of course the same kind of master-rhetorician as Shrike—opposing to Christ "Not force, but well-couched fraud, well-woven snares" (1.97) by "the persuasive rhetoric/That sleeked his tongue" (4.4–5)—but in the end he, too, is profoundly disconcerted by Christ's immovability.

The thematic reduction that this alignment of Miss Lonelyhearts with Christ and of Shrike with Satan immediately suggests, however, is absurd. As John R. May contends, this reading makes Shrike a Satan-figure who tempts Miss Lonelyhearts to presumption ("The rock is the sign of Miss Lonelyhearts's presumption; it is a traditional image for the unchanging fidelity of God"),

From *American Apocalypses: The Image of the End of the World in American Literature.* © 1985 by the Johns Hopkins University Press.

and if Miss Lonelyhearts is punished for that presumption with death, Shrike's victory signals the "last loosening of Satan," or impending apocalypse.

That this is a false reduction of the novel is evident in West's insistence on aligning his antagonists the other way as well: Shrike, after all—whose name is a near-anagram of Christ—is the one who keeps talking about Christ; and while his is a devastating rhetoric in which the *real* alternative of Christ is destroyed, that rhetoric *becomes* his image of order, his rock, which guarantees his invulnerability throughout the novel. If Milton's Christ throughout *Paradise Regained* remains "unmoved," then Shrike is clearly the dominant Christ figure here; for Shrike is unmoved by the suffering that Miss Lonelyhearts perceives precisely because he can retreat into the illusory world of rhetoric, a paradoxical discovery of order in absence that significantly parallels Christ's own deferral of presential order to an absent future. Shrike's rhetoric, for Miss Lonelyhearts, represents a temptation to order analogous to Betty's more naive belief in order, as well as to his own hopeless wishing for an apocalypse—all temptations he knows he must stay away from, for they will only exacerbate his sickness. Miss Lonelyhearts is driven throughout the novel by an acute perception of suffering that simply will not reduce either to Betty's simplicities or to Shrike's rhetorical sophistication:

> A man is hired to give advice to the readers of a newspaper [he explains to Betty]. The job is a circulation stunt and the whole staff considers it a joke. He welcomes the job, for it might lead to a gossip column, and anyway he's tired of being a leg man. He too considers the job a joke, but after several months at it, the joke begins to escape him. He sees that the majority of the letters are profoundly humble pleas for moral and spiritual advice, that they are inarticulate expressions of genuine suffering. He also discovers that his correspondents take him seriously. For the first time in his life, he is forced to examine the values by which he lives. This examination shows him that he is the victim of the joke and not its perpetrator.

If Milton's Christ represents order and Satan a restless wandering through chaos, clearly West aligns Miss Lonelyhearts with the latter. Miss Lonelyhearts is restless throughout the novel because he sees too well that all order, indeed all *language*, is a wholly unjustified reduction of the human truth of suffering to nonexistence. As a newspaper writer, he deals in words and is taught to manipulate words by his feature editor, Shrike; but that manipulation soon goes sour on him. The letters he receives are "inarticulate expressions of genuine suffering"—which is to say that genuine suffering exposes the reductive dangers of articulation, for to articulate suffering in his responses to the letters is always to falsify the suffering.

West's problem, of course, is that he is writing a novel about the inauthenticity of articulation. His novel launches a powerful assault on the entire Western tradition of the apocalyptic unveiling of order, but by doing so *verbally*, it partakes in the very tradition that West attacks. This is, of course, the central dilemma in American writing: How does one forge an order that will not harden into a rock of repression? By what authority can one destroy all authoritarian images of order? Miss Lonelyhearts undergoes his negative revelation in the end, gives in to the temptation to become "proof against all temptation," and becomes the rock: "He approached Betty with a smile, for his mind was free and clear. The things that muddied it had precipitated out into the rock." But schizophrenia (which we may define as a form of ethical splitting, perhaps) is no answer to the writer's dilemma. Having devalued the apocalyptic transformation of chaos into order, he must seek a new transformation, a new reduction, perhaps, but one that will not falsify the chaotic facts of inarticulate human existence.

Early in the novel, Miss Lonelyhearts has a sudden memory from childhood that seems to offer West a tentative way out:

> One winter evening, he had been waiting with his little sister for their father to come home from church. She was eight years old then, and he was twelve. Made sad by the pause between playing and eating, he had gone to the piano and had begun a piece by Mozart. It was the first time he had ever voluntarily gone to the piano. His sister left her picture book to dance to his music. She had never danced before. She danced gravely and carefully, a simply dance yet formal. . . . As Miss Lonelyhearts stood at the bar, swaying slightly to the remembered music, he thought of children dancing. Square replacing oblong and being replaced by circle. Every child, everywhere; in the whole world there was not one child who was not gravely, sweetly dancing. (ellipsis West's)

Miss Lonelyhearts quickly dismisses his memory — "What in Christ's name was this Christ business? And children gravely dancing? He would ask Shrike to be transferred to the sports department." But the dance remains a possibility — a possible reduction of flux to order in which order is ephemeral, always passing away: "Square replacing oblong and being replaced by circle." The being-replaced of the dance is Yeats's Romantic image for art, of course, repeated in Eliot's *Four Quartets* as "the still point of the turning world."

But West, as opposed to Yeats and Eliot, remains profoundly mistrustful of that image; the image, too, West understands, is a falsification of the inarticulate flux of human suffering.

Chronology

1903	Born Nathan Weinstein, in New York City on October 17, son of Anna Wallenstein Weinstein and Max Weinstein, a building contractor, both born in Russia.
1920	After three poor academic years, leaves DeWitt Clinton High School without graduating.
1921	Enters Tufts College in September, using a forged high school transcript.
1922	Transfers to Brown University, apparently on the strength of another student's transcript.
1924	Graduates from Brown University in June, with a B.A. in English.
1926–1927	Lives in Paris, October—January. Legally changes name to Nathanael West.
1931	*The Dream Life of Balso Snell.*
1932	Edits "little magazine," *Contact*, with William Carlos Williams. Publishes early versions of *Miss Lonelyhearts*.
1933	*Miss Lonelyhearts* published, but publisher's bankruptcy prevents wide availability of the book. Works as contract scriptwriter in Hollywood for Columbia Studios.
1934	*A Cool Million.*
1936	Scriptwriter for Republic Studios, later for R.K.O. and Universal.
1939	*The Day of the Locust.*
1940	Marries Eileen McKenney on April 19 in Beverly Hills, California. Killed with his wife in an automobile accident on December 22 near El Centro, California.

Contributors

HAROLD BLOOM, Sterling Professor of the Humanities at Yale University, is the author of *The Anxiety of Influence, Poetry and Repression,* and many other volumes of literary criticism. A MacArthur Prize Fellow, he is the general editor of *The Chelsea House Library of Literary Criticism.*

STANLEY EDGAR HYMAN was Professor of Literature at Bennington College. His books include *The Tangled Bank* and *The Armed Vision.*

ROGER D. ABRAHAMS is Professor of English and Anthropology at the University of Texas at Austin. His many works include *Between the Living and the Dead, Performers, Performances and Enactments* and *The Man-of-Words in the West Indies.* He is also coeditor of *Afro-American Folk Culture: An Annotated Bibliography, Counting Out Rhymes: A Dictionary,* and *After Africa.*

MARCUS SMITH, Professor of English at Loyola University, New Orleans, has written numerous articles on modern American literature.

JOHN R. MAY is Professor of English at Louisiana State University, Baton Rouge. He has written essays on film, religion, and culture; his books include *The Pruning Word: The Parables of Flannery O'Connor* and *Toward a New Earth.*

JAMES W. HICKEY has written books on Nathanael West and psychoanalytic criticism.

JEFFREY L. DUNCAN teaches at Eastern Michigan University. He has written on Emerson and Thoreau, and is the author of *The Metaphor of the Word in Nineteenth-Century American Literature.*

MARTIN TROPP, Assistant Professor of English at Babson College, is the author of *Mary Shelley's Monster: The Story of Frankenstein.*

MARK CONROY is Assistant Professor of English at Ohio State University and the author of *Modernism and Authority,* a study of Flaubert and Conrad.

131

DOUGLAS ROBINSON, Associate Professor of English Philology at the University of Tampere in Finland, is the author of *John Barth's Giles Goat-Boy: A Study* and *American Apocalypses*.

Bibliography

Aaron, Daniel. "Late Thoughts on Nathanael West." *Massachusetts Review* 6 (1965): 307–16.

Andreach, Robert J. "Nathanael West's Miss Lonelyhearts: Between the Dead Pan and the Unborn Christ." *Modern Fiction Studies* 12 (1966): 251–66.

Auden, W. H. "West's Disease." In *The Dyer's Hand,* 238–45. New York: Random House, 1962.

Brown, Daniel R. "The War within Nathanael West: Naturalism and Existentialism." *Modern Fiction Studies* 2 (1974): 181–202.

Bush, C. W. "This Stupendous Fabric: The Metaphysics of Order in Melville's *Pierre* and Nathanael West's *Miss Lonelyhearts. Journal of American Studies* 1, no. 2 (1967): 269–74.

Comerchero, Victor. *Nathanael West: The Ironic Prophet.* Syracuse, N.Y.: Syracuse University Press, 1964.

Cramer, Carter M. *The World of Nathanael West.* Emporia, Kansas: Emporia State Research Studies, 1971.

Edenbaum, Robert I. "Dada and Surrealism in the United States: A Literary Instance." *Arts in Society* 5 (1968): 114–25.

Fiedler, Leslie A. *Love and Death in the American Novel.* New York: Stein & Day, 1966.

Frank, Mike. "The Passion of Miss Lonelyhearts According to Nathanael West." *Studies in Short Fiction* 10 (1973): 67–74.

Geha, Richard, Jr. "*Miss Lonelyhearts:* A Dual Mission of Mercy." *University of Hartford Studies in Literature* 3 (1971): 116–31.

Hand, Nancy Walker. "A Novel in the Form of a Comic Strip: Nathanael West's *Miss Lonelyhearts.*" *The Serif* 5, no. 2 (June 1968): 14–21.

Hollis, C. Carol. "Nathanael West and Surrealist Violence." *Fresco* 7 (Fall 1957): 5–21.

Jackson, Thomas H., ed. *Twentieth-Century Interpretations of* Miss Lonelyhearts. Englewood Cliffs, N.J.: Prentice-Hall, 1971.

Klein, Marcus. "Nathan Weinstein and Nathanael West." In *Foreigners: The Making of American Literature 1900–1940,* 249–69. Chicago: University of Chicago Press, 1981.

Laurenson, Diane and Alan Swingewood. "Alienation, Reification and the Novel: Sartre, Camus, Nathanael West." In *The Sociology of Literature,* 237–45. London: Rowman, 1978.

Lewis, R. W. B. "Days of Wrath and Laughter." In *Trials of the Word: Essays in American*

Literature and the Humanistic Tradition, 212–18. New Haven: Yale University Press. 1965.

Light, James F. *Nathanael West: An Interpretive Study.* Evanston, Ill.: Northwestern University Press, 1961.

Madden, David, ed. *Nathanael West: The Cheaters and the Cheated.* Deland, Fla.: Everett/ Edwards, 1973.

Malin, Irving. *Nathanael West's Novels.* Carbondale: Southern Illinois University Press, 1972.

Martin, Jay. *Nathanael West: The Art of His Life.* New York: Farrar, Straus & Giroux, 1970.

————, ed. *Nathanael West: A Collection of Critical Essays.* Englewood Cliffs, N.J.: Prentice-Hall, 1971.

Nelson, Gerald B. "Lonelyhearts." In *Ten Versions of America,* 77–90. New York: Knopf, 1972.

Olsen, Bruce. "Nathanael West: The Use of Cynicism." In *Minor American Novelists,* edited by Charles Alva Hoyt, 81–94. Carbondale: Southern Illinois University Press, 1970.

Orvell, Miles D. "The Messianic Sexuality in *Miss Lonelyhearts.*" *Studies in Short Fiction* 2, vol. 10 (1973).

Perry, Robert M. *Nathanael West's Miss Lonelyhearts.* New York: Seabury Press, 1969.

Podhoretz, Norman. "Nathanael West: A Particular Kind of Joking." In *Doings and Undoings: The Fifties and After in American Writing,* 65–75. New York: Farrar, Straus & Giroux, 1964.

Pritchett, V. S. *"Miss Lonelyhearts."* In *The Living Novel and Later Appreciations,* 276–82. New York: Random House, 1968.

Reid, Randall. *The Fiction of Nathanael West: No Redeemer, No Promised Land.* Chicago: The University of Chicago Press, 1967.

Richardson, Robert D. *"Miss Lonelyhearts."* *The University Review* 33, no. 2 (1966): 151–57.

Ross, Alan. "The Dead Center: An Introduction to Nathanael West." In *The Complete Works of Nathanael West,* vii–xxii. New York: Farrar, Straus & Giroux, 1957.

Schoenewolf, Carroll. "Jamesian Psychology and Nathanael West's *Miss Lonelyhearts.*" *San Jose Studies* 7, no. 3 (1981): 80–86.

Schulz, Max F. *Radical Sophistication: Studies in Contemporary Jewish-American Novelists.* Athens: Ohio University Press, 1969, 36–55.

Scott, Nathan A., Jr. *Nathanael West.* Grand Rapids, Mich.: Eerdmans, 1971.

Shelton, Frank W. "Nathanael West and the Theatre of the Absurd: A Comparative Study." *Southern Humanities Review* 10 (1976): 225–34.

Symons, Julian. "The Case of Nathanael West." In *Critical Occasions,* 99–105. London: Hamish Hamilton, 1966.

Tibbets, A. M. "The Strange Half-World of Nathanael West." *The Prairie Schooner* 34, no. 1 (1960): 8–14.

Tuch, Ronald. "The Dismantled Self in the Fiction of Nathanael West." *Psychocultural Review* 1 (1977): 43–48.

Vannatta, Dennis P. *Nathanael West: An Annotated Bibliography of the Scholarship and Works.* New York: Garland Publishing, 1976.

White, William. *Nathanael West: A Comprehensive Bibliography.* Kent, Ohio: Kent State University Press, 1975.

Widmer, Kingsley. "The Sweet, Savage Prophecies of Nathanael West." In *The Thirties,* edited by Warren French. Deland, Fla.: Everett/Edwards, 1967.

Acknowledgments

"*Miss Lonelyhearts*" (originally entitled "Nathanael West") by Stanley Edgar Hyman from *University of Minnesota Pamphlets on American Writers,* © 1962 by the University of Minnesota. Reprinted by permission of the University of Minnesota Press.

"Religious Experience in *Miss Lonelyhearts*") by Marcus Smith from *Contemporary Literature* 9, no. 2 (Spring 1968), © 1968 by the Regents of the University of Wisconsin. Reprinted by permission of the University of Wisconsin Press.

"Words and Deeds" by John R. May from *Toward a New Earth: Apocalypse in the American Novel* by John R. May, © 1972 by the University of Notre Dame Press. Reprinted by permission.

"Freudian Criticism and *Miss Lonelyhearts*" by James W. Hickey from *Nathanael West: The Cheaters and the Cheated,* edited by David Madden, © 1973 by David Madden. Reprinted by permission of Everett/Edwards, Inc.

"The Problem of Language in *Miss Lonelyhearts*" by Jeffrey L. Duncan from *The Iowa Review* 8, no. 1 (Winter 1977), © 1977 by the University of Iowa. Reprinted by permission of the author and *The Iowa Review.*

"Nathanael West and the Persistence of Hope" by Martin Tropp from *Renascence* 31, no. 4 (Summer 1979), © 1979 by the Catholic Renascence Society, Inc. Reprinted by permission.

"Letters and Spirit in *Miss Lonelyhearts*" by Mark Conroy from *The University of Windsor Review* 17, no. 1 (Fall/Winter 1982), © 1982 by the University of Windsor Review. Reprinted by permission.

"The Ritual Icon" by Douglas Robinson from *American Apocalypses: The Image of the End of the World in American Literature* by Douglas Robinson, © 1985 by the Johns Hopkins University Press. Reprinted by permission.

"Androgynes Bound: Nathanael West's *Miss Lonelyhearts*" by Roger D. Abrahams from *Seven Contemporary Authors,* edited by Thomas B. Whitbread, © 1966 by the University of Texas Press. Reprinted by permission.

Index